Frontiers of Forensic Science

Innovation, Technology, and Justice

nova
science publishers
www.novapublishers.com
New York

Criminal Justice, Law Enforcement and Corrections

More information about this series can be found at

Cybercrime and Cybersecurity Research

More information about this series can be found at

Walid M. Khalilia
Editor

Frontiers of Forensic Science

Innovation, Technology, and Justice

nova
science publishers
www.novapublishers.com
New York

DOI: https://doi.org/10.52305/OIDG0672

Library of Congress Cataloging-in-Publication Data

ISBN: 979-8-90134-160-5 (Softcover)
ISBN: 979-8-90134-221-3 (eBook)

Published by Nova Science Publishers, Inc. † New York

Contents

Preface

Where science meets justice and the future is now

Frontiers of Forensic Science: Innovation, Technology, and Justice offers an in-depth, forward-looking look at the groundbreaking developments transforming the field today. Bringing together insights from multiple disciplines, it connects emerging technologies, new approaches to biological evidence, and how justice is ultimately served.

The book begins by looking ahead to the future of experimentation in digital forensics, tackling key issues such as the growing role of artificial intelligence (AI), machine and deep learning in solving cybercrimes. It also dives into the legal and ethical challenges surrounding AI-related crimes, exploring how justice systems are adapting to new autonomous technologies and the difficulties of determining who should be held responsible. On the biological side, it introduces ear-prints as a novel form of forensic evidence, examining both their promise and the current hurdles in using them for criminal identification.

Looking at the social side of forensic science, the book shines a light on the overlooked experiences of male victims, and calls for more gender-neutral and inclusive practices to ensure every victim receives fair recognition and treatment. It wraps up with a detailed look at forensic spectral analysis, highlighting advanced techniques such as infrared, Raman, and mass spectrometry, along with AI-powered data interpretation, all of which are helping to improve how evidence is detected and analyzed.

Frontiers of Forensic Science is an essential resource for forensic professionals, forensic scientists and researchers, legal experts, students and educators and technology professionals, who refuse to be left behind. It is a must read for anyone dedicated to using innovation and technology to push the boundaries of justice in today's fast-changing world.

This book is an important resource for contemporary investigation and legal procedures to understanding the ways in which technology, law, and science interact.

About the Editor

Dr. Walid M. Khalilia
Forensic Science Dep., Al-Istiqlal University, Jericho, Palestine
Email: walidkhalilia@gmail.com
https://orcid.org/0000-0001-8952-5628

Dr. Khalilia is a full Professor in Forensic Biology at AlIstiqlal University. He is an active researcher who works in the fields of Forensic Science, Cell Biology, Molecular Biology, Environmental Radiobiology, and Educational studies.

Dr. Khalilia served in different positions at Al-Istiqlal University: Vice president for academic affairs, Dean of Graduate Studies and Scientific Research, and chairperson of forensic science department. Chairperson of Al-Istiqlal University Research Journal Council. He is the Founder and Chairman of Forensic Science Department at Al-Istiqlal University. Dr. Khalilia has many peer-reviewed articles in international journals, and participation in international conferences, in addition to supervisor of many scientific research projects. He acts as an editorial board member and reviewer for many international journals, managing and implementing projects with a high level of professionalism. In addition, he is an active member in many national and international scientific societies. He is a premier member of Arab Society for Forensic Science and Forensic Medicine (ASFSFM), founding member of

Palestinian Society of Biological Sciences (PSBS), and member of European Association for Cancer Research (EACR).

Dr. Khalilia Awards the Scientific Research Award for the year 2022, from the Palestinian Ministry of Higher Studies and Scientific Research for his scientific research in the field of the COVID-19 epidemic. Moreover, he awards a visiting research fellowship from the Palestinian Quebec Science Bridge (PQSB), in project entitled "Interpretation of Forensic Biological Evidence: Towards a New Model in Palestine," in Université du Québec à Trois-Rivières, Quebec, Canada. 2023.

Chapter 1

The Future of Experimentation in Digital Forensics

Edson OliveiraJr*
Informatics Department, State University of Maringá (UEM), Maringá-PR, Brazil

Abstract

Digital Forensics (DF) focuses on identifying, acquiring, analyzing, and reporting information from digital devices, especially in computer crime investigations. The investigative process encompasses phases of identification, preservation, collection, examination, analysis, and presentation, all of which are crucial for maintaining evidence of integrity and ensuring legal admissibility. The rise of complex digital environments, such as cloud computing and the Internet of Things (IoT), along with technologies like Artificial Intelligence (AI) and Natural Language Processing (NLP), is reshaping the field. This chapter emphasizes the importance of experimentation in developing and validating DF methodologies. Reliable forensic findings are tied to rigorous experimental processes. Challenges include a lack of standardization, insufficient documentation of experimental elements, and limited realistic datasets for validating forensic tools. Additionally, current forensic tools often lack benchmarking frameworks. To enhance controlled experimentation in DF, the chapter advocates for developing support tools for planning and conducting experiments, fostering openness for reproducibility, and strategically integrating AI and Machine Learning (ML). It also emphasizes the importance of formal experimental designs, adherence to standards, quality assurance, and addressing emerging challenges to advance the field.

---

* Corresponding Author's Email: edson@din.uem.br

In: Frontiers of Forensic Science: Innovation, Technology, and Justice
Editor: Walid M. Khalilia
ISBN: 979-8-90134-160-5

Keywords: artificial intelligence, digital forensics, experimentation, reproducibility, standardization

Introduction

The field of Digital Forensics (DF) plays an increasingly vital role in today's society. It focuses on the identification, acquisition, analysis, and reporting of information found on digital devices, particularly in the context of investigating computer crimes. This discipline provides essential methodologies and techniques for systematically examining digital media, uncovering relevant evidence, and ensuring the integrity of that evidence so it can be considered admissible in legal proceedings. As our lives become increasingly intertwined with digital technologies, the demand for robust and reliable digital forensic practices continues to grow, underscoring the importance of this field in maintaining security and administering justice (Padma and Don, 2022).

The investigative process within DF is typically structured around a set of well-defined and rigorous phases (Palmer, 2001). These phases generally include identification of the digital artifacts and discovery of evidence related to an incident; preservation of the evi- dence through appropriate classification to prevent loss or damage; collection of the nec- essary digital media; examination and analysis to identify relevant information, data, or activities; and finally, presentation of the organized and documented findings to the compe- tent authorities. Maintaining a strict chain of custody throughout these phases is mandatory to ensure the credibility and reliability of digital evidence.

However, the landscape of DF is continuously changing due to the rapid growth of complex digital environments, such as cloud computing and the Internet of Things (IoT). Additionally, the increasing use of advanced technologies, such as Artificial Intelligence (AI) and Natural Language Processing (NLP), in various aspects of our digital lives presents both opportunities and challenges for forensic investigators. These evolving technologies and digital environments create new complexities related to data storage, virtualization, jurisdictional issues, and the vast amounts of information that must be analyzed. As a result, traditional forensic methods are often rendered less effective.

In this dynamic context, experimentation in DF becomes paramount (OliveiraJr et al., 2020, OliveiraJr et al., 2021, OliveiraJr et al., 2022, Silva et al., 2025). It is essential to develop, validate, and refine methodologies and tools for effectively and reliably acquiring, examining, analyzing, and reporting digital evidence. Ensuring that forensic findings are both reliable and legally defensible directly depends on the rigor and reproducibility of the underlying experimental processes. High-quality experimentation enables researchers and practitioners to evaluate the effectiveness of various approaches, identify potential limitations, and propose necessary improvements, ultimately strengthening the foundation of digital forensic science.

This chapter focuses on the future of experimentation in DF. It will explore the current challenges facing the field, including standardization, documentation, and the availability of realistic testing environments. Furthermore, it will delve into prospective actions and strategies aimed at enhancing the rigor, reproducibility, and efficiency of controlled experiments. These include the leveraging of support tooling, embracing open science principles, and strategically integrating AI and Machine Learning (ML) to pave the way for more robust and credible digital forensic investigations.

Basics of Digital Forensics

DF is the field that involves the identification, acquisition, analysis, and reporting of information found on digital devices, often in the context of computer crime investigations. It encompasses a variety of techniques and methodologies to systematically examine digital media and ensure the integrity of evidence, making it admissible in legal proceedings (Solanke and Biasiotti, 2022).

The investigative process in DF typically involves well-defined and rigorous phases, including identification, preservation, collection, examination, analysis, and presentation (Palmer, 2001) (Figure 1). In the identification phase, the artifact is identified, and evidence related to the incident is discovered. During the collection phase, the necessary measures are taken to classify and preserve the evidence, thereby preventing potential loss or damage to the digital device (Raghavan, 2013). Next, processes are applied in the organization phase, which includes the examination and analysis phases, to identify relevant information, data, or activities in the evidence (Mir et al., 2016). Examples of analyses performed to reconstruct the events that caused the incident include data mining, encryption and decryption, and peer-to-peer network analysis, among others (Martini and Choo, 2012). Finally, the data is organized and documented appropriately in the preservation phase, allowing it to be presented to the competent authorities in the case (John, 2012).

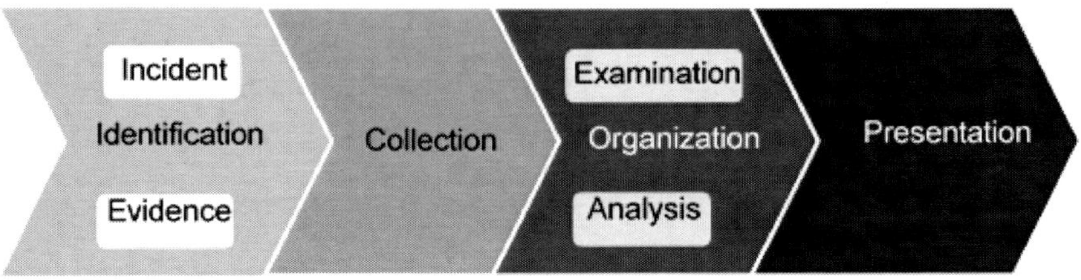

Figure 1. The DF investigative process phases (Palmer, 2001).

These phases are crucial for maintaining the credibility and reliability of digital evidence (Blancaflor et al., 2023).

D encompasses several subareas, each focusing on different aspects of digital evidence (Tiwari et al., 2021), including:

1. Computer Forensics: Deals with data found on computers and storage devices;
2. Network Forensics: Involves monitoring and analyzing network traffic to detect and investigate security incidents;
3. Mobile Device Forensics: Focuses on recovering digital evidence from mobile devices like smartphones and tablets;
4. Cloud Forensics: Pertains to the investigation of data stored in cloud computing environments; and
5. IoT Forensics: Concerns the extraction and analysis of data from the IoT devices.

Each subarea presents unique challenges and requires specialized tools and methodologies (Tiwari et al., 2021).

Computer Forensics is a specialized subarea of DF that primarily deals with data found on computers and storage devices. This field is crucial for investigating incidents involving computer systems and their associated storage media, aiming to identify, preserve, collect, examine, and analyze relevant information in the context of computer crime investigations (Tiwari et al., 2021). Network Forensics focuses on monitoring and analyzing network traffic to detect and investigate security incidents. Its primary objective is to reconstruct events and identify malicious or anomalous activities occurring within a network infrastructure. This includes examining communication patterns, hierarchies, and connections between devices, which techniques like network and graph analysis can facilitate (Cook et al., 2023). Mobile Device Forensics is a specialized area of DF focused on recovering digital evidence from mobile devices, including smartphones and tablets. The continuous proliferation of these devices, along with the broader IoT landscape, introduces significant new complexities and challenges for digital forensic investigators (Salem et al., 2023).

In recent years, the proliferation of IoT devices has introduced new complexities to DF (Salem et al., 2023). IoT forensics involves collecting and analyzing data from interconnected devices, which often have limited storage and processing capabilities. The diversity and ubiquity of these devices necessitate novel approaches to evidence acquisition and analysis. Cloud computing has also transformed the landscape of DF. Cloud forensics necessitates investigators to navigate distributed data storage, virtualized environments, and jurisdictional complexities, rendering traditional forensic methods less effective. Researchers have been developing frameworks to address these challenges and ensure the integrity of cloud-based evidence (Masud et al., 2021). Integrating AI into DF has been a significant development. AI techniques are being utilized to automate the analysis of large datasets, identify patterns, and enhance the accuracy of forensic investigations. However, adopting AI also raises concerns about the transparency and explain ability of forensic processes (Casino et al., 2022). NLP has emerged as a valuable DF and cybersecurity tool. NLP-based systems can analyze textual data to detect anomalies, identify threats, and assist in investigating cybercrimes. The application of NLP facilitates the processing of vast amounts of unstructured data, enhancing the efficiency of forensic analyses (Ukwen and Karabatak, 2021).

The reliability of DF methods heavily depends on the availability of realistic datasets for testing and validation. The scarcity of such datasets poses challenges for researchers in evaluating the effectiveness of forensic tools and techniques. Discussions around the realism of datasets are crucial for advancing the field and ensuring the applicability of research outcomes (Göbel et al., 2023).

Reproducibility is a cornerstone of scientific research, including DF (Costa et al., 2024). Ensuring that forensic methods yield consistent results across different studies is vital for establishing credibility. Researchers have been exploring tools and methodologies to enhance reproducibility in computational research, addressing challenges such as data variability and methodological transparency.

The DF community has been actively addressing the challenges associated with reproducibility. Efforts include the development of standardized evaluation methods and optimization techniques to ensure that AI models used in forensic investigations produce consistent and reliable results (Solanke and Biasiotti, 2022).

Empirical studies are crucial in advancing DF by providing evidence-based evaluations of forensic tools and methodologies. Such studies contribute to the development of best practices and inform the creation of guidelines that enhance the reliability of forensic investigations (Beebe, 2009).

Controlled experiments are crucial for evaluating the performance of forensic tools under diverse conditions (OliveiraJr et al., 2020). They enable researchers to systematically evaluate the effectiveness of different approaches, identify potential limitations, and propose improvements. This rigorous scientific approach ensures that forensic methods are both reliable and valid.

The integration of reproducibility measures into scholarly research is gaining attention. Incorporating replicability indicators into academic search systems can help researchers identify studies that adhere to high standards of scientific rigor, thereby promoting transparency and trust in research findings (Wu et al., 2024).

Addressing reproducibility challenges, often referred to as "reproducibility debt," is crucial for advancing DF. By acknowledging and addressing these challenges, the forensic research community can enhance the credibility of its findings and ensure that forensic methods are robust and dependable (Hassan et al., 2024).

Controlled Experimentation in Digital Forensics

Experimentation in DF is essential for developing, validating, and refining methods used to acquire, examine, analyze, and report digital evidence. This process ensures that forensic findings are both reliable and legally defensible. However, the field faces significant challenges related to the standardization and documentation of experimental procedures, which can impede the reproducibility and reliability of research outcomes.

A systematic mapping study analyzing 107 primary studies revealed that many DF experiments lack proper documentation of essential elements, including hypotheses, variables, experimental design, instrumentation, validity evaluation, setup, training, datasets, benchmarks, statistical techniques, and limitations. This deficiency hampers the reproducibility and reliability of experimental results in DF (OliveiraJr et al., 2022).

To address these issues, frameworks and conceptual models have been proposed to guide researchers in conducting rigorous and reproducible experiments. For instance, a conceptual model, ExperDF-CM, has been developed to assist DF researchers in planning, executing, analyzing, and disseminating experiments. This model emphasizes the importance of proper documentation and sharing of experimental data to promote reproducibility and trust in digital forensic research.

Integrating AI and ML into DF experimentation has emerged as a promising avenue to enhance the efficiency and accuracy of investigations (Dunsin et al., 2024). AI and ML techniques have been applied to various domains within DF, including data collection and recovery, cybercrime timeline reconstruction, big data analysis, pattern recognition, and incident response. However, adopting these technologies is still in its early stages, necessitating further research to fully harness their potential.

In Digital Multimedia Forensics (DMF), experimentation plays a pivotal role in validating techniques for authenticating and analyzing images, audio, and video. A review of 49 experiments in DMF revealed that many studies lack comprehensive reporting on experimental elements, including hypotheses, variables, and data-sharing practices (OliveiraJr et al., 2021). This gap highlights the need for enhanced documentation to improve the reproducibility and reliability of DMF research.

To further promote rigorous experimentation, conceptual models and ontologies have been proposed to standardize the planning, execution, and dissemination of DF experiments (OliveiraJr et al., 2020, Silva et al., 2025). They aim to provide a structured framework that encapsulates the essential components of an experiment, facilitating better documentation, data sharing, and replication of studies within the DF community. The following sections provide an overview of how DF experimentation has been formalized using conceptual models and ontologies.

The ExperDF-CM Conceptual Model

OliveiraJr et al. (2020) developed a conceptual model to support the documentation, planning, execution, and dissemination of evidence in the DF experimentation process, known as the Experimentation in DF Conceptual Model (ExperDF-CM). This model was built based on a secondary study

(OliveiraJr et al., 2022), which analyzed over 200 experiments in the DF domain. A substantial amount of data was extracted from these studies, which informed the derivation of the model. ExperDF-CM is grounded in the stages of the experimentation process outlined by (Wohlin et al., 2012) and provides a structured overview of a DF-controlled experiment.

ExperDF-CM is a static data model that represents knowledge through a map composed of rectangles and connecting lines. The authors selected a semantic-based knowledge model due to the specific characteristics of the DF experimentation domain.

The ExperDF-CM concepts consider the key elements found in the analyzed experiments conducted on DF research topics (OliveiraJr et al., 2022). DF experiments aim to establish a cause-and-effect relationship based on a theory and real-world observations through the application of treatments and subsequent outcomes. To do so, four different stages are considered:

1. *Planning,* which is responsible for providing more control to the experiment by previously defining, for instance, the goal, hypothesis, instruments, and variables;
2. *Operation,* which executes the experiment according to its planning, mainly by collecting data with pre-defined instruments;
3. *Analysis and interpretation,* which provides data analysis mainly based on observed data (samples), such as descriptive statistics, normality, and hypothesis testing;
4. *Reporting,* responsible for disseminating the experiment planning, operation, analysis, and interpretation to interested audiences, such as researchers and industry practitioners.

Figure 2 presents the overall view of the conceptual model.

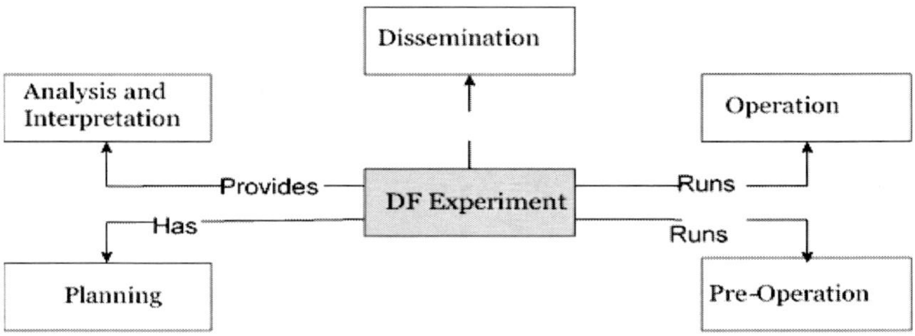

Figure 2. ExperDF-CM main concepts (OliveiraJr et al., 2020).

Each central concept is described as follows:

- *DF Experiment:* is the DF experiment itself. A DF Experiment *has* a relationship with planning and *runs* operation. It *provides* analysis and interpretation, as well as *reports* dissemination;
- *Planning:* represents the planning stage of DF experimentation;
- *Pre-Operation:* is a set of procedures run before beginning the experiment operation itself;
- *Operation:* concept representing the operation stage of an experiment, most related to data collection;
- *Analysis and Interpretation:* concept related to statistical analysis techniques and limitations; and
- *Dissemination:* encompasses reporting experiments and provides a way to increase the reproducibility of DF experiments.

As ExperDF-CM is an abstract view of fundamental concepts involved in a DF-controlled experiment, experimenters require a more formalized model to specify such concepts. To do so, (Silva et al., 2025) developed the ExperDF-Onto ontology, which is described next.

The ExperDF-Onto Ontology

The goal of ExperDF-Onto (Silva et al., 2025) is to establish a clear conceptualization of DF controlled experiments, detailing the main concepts, properties, and relationships involved. ExperDF-Onto is designed to standardize terminology, enhance information retrieval, analyze entities, model crime scenarios in DF, and support DF experts in decision-making during evidence analysis. It assists in several key areas:

1. *Data Semantics Assignment:* it accurately describes digital artifacts;
2. *Chain of Custody Modeling:* it ensures the registration, traceability, and integrity of data;
3. *Temporal and Timeline Analysis:* it enables the creation of precise sequences of events;
4. *Network and Graph Analysis:* it facilitates the modeling and analysis of complex connections between communication patterns, hierarchies, and devices.

Overall, ExperDF-Onto is a valuable tool for improving the effectiveness of DF investigations.

ExperDF-Onto was developed using ExperDF-CM as its foundation. The ExperDF-CM was not only reused but also refined to create the ontology. This conceptual model provided a crucial starting point, offering a high-level overview of the concepts to be represented. It served as an initial reference from which a more detailed model was created. This new model included specific design elements that addressed computational and technical forensic considerations.

To develop the ExperDF-Onto, each higher-level concept from the ExperDF-CM was represented as an ontology module. The concepts from ExperDF-CM were depicted as UML classes and further refined. Attributes were incorporated into these classes to provide characterization, and new courses were created to address aspects that were not covered in the ExperDF-CM.

Figure 3 illustrates the ExperDF-Onto architecture. For each higher-level concept in ExperDF-CM, we have defined a corresponding module. In the figure, each package represents an ontology module. A dependency relationship between two packages indicates that the source module reuses concepts from the target module.

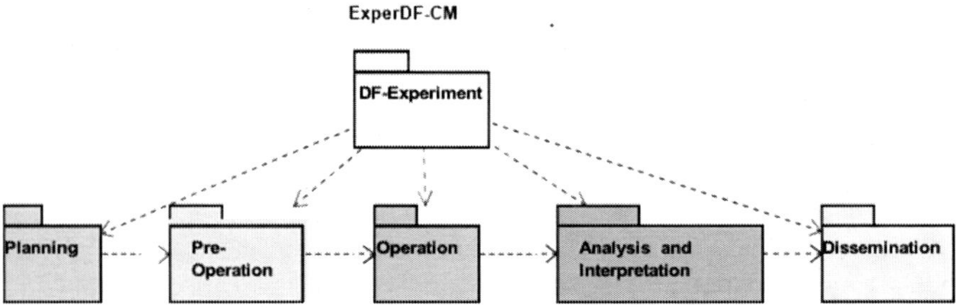

Figure 3. ExperDF-Onto - Architecture (Silva et al., 2025).

ExperDF-Onto is quite extensive. We present fragments that illustrate scenarios. These scenarios relate to specific competence questions (questions that the ontology should be able to answer) and have been selected to help readers understand how to interpret and utilize the ontology elements during each phase of DF.

When planning an experiment, one should consider *"what elements need to be documented to plan a DF experiment rigorously?"* Figure 4 shows some ontology classes related to experiment planning.

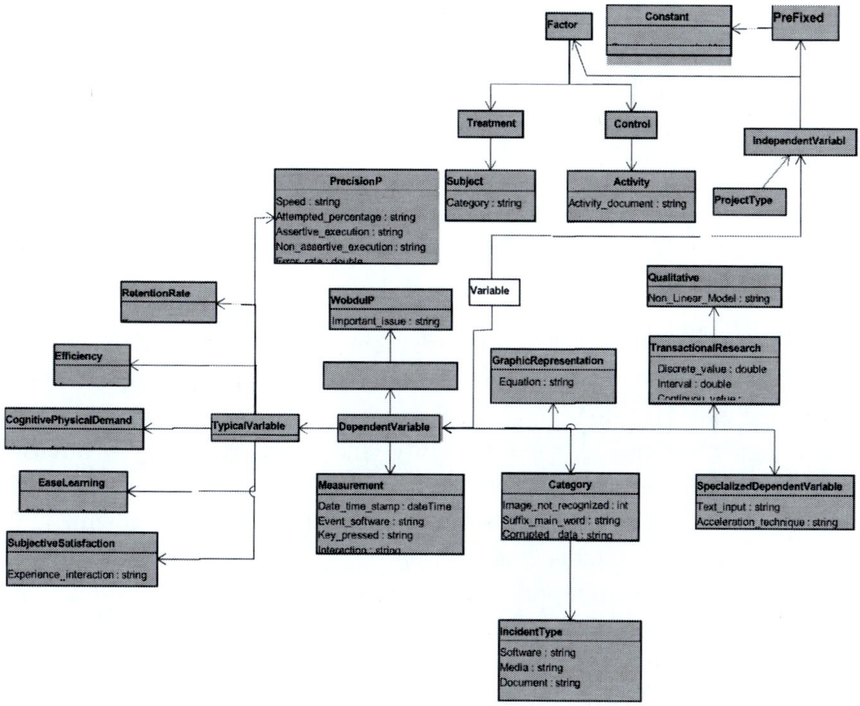

Figure 4. ExperDF-Onto excerpt for the DF-controlled experiment in the phase planning phase regarding selecting Variables (Silva et al., 2025).

For example, the class Variable acts as either an independent or a dependent variable, each fulfilling distinct roles. The class Independent Variable can be associated with either a pre-defined value or the treatments and controls.

An example of a scenario could involve someone contemplating "*the best way to measure a dependent variable.*" The independent variable also plays a crucial role in this consideration. Efficiency and precision are widely used metrics for dependent variables in DF experiments (OliveiraJr et al., 2022). These variables are influenced by the type of incident (IncidentType) occurring in the experiment, such as at the software level.

The complete ExperDF-Onto specification, application examples, and SPARQL queries are in (Silva et al., 2025).

Prospective Actions for Digital Forensics Controlled Experimentation

This section presents actionable elements for the future of controlled experimentation in DF.

Support Tooling

Planning, conducting, and disseminating controlled experiments in DF can significantly benefit from software tools in several ways. Tools should assist in designing experiments by providing templates, checklists, and predefined methodologies to ensure reproducibility and compliance with forensic standards. Additionally, simulation tools enable researchers to model various attack scenarios and forensic investigation techniques before implementing them in the real world (Balon et al., 2021).

During data collection and experiment execution, automated tools can capture and log system activities, network traffic, and forensic artifacts in a controlled environment, thereby reducing human error and improving accuracy. Virtualized environments and testbeds enable the safe execution of experiments without risking live systems or compromising the integrity of evidence. Scripting and automation tools allow repetitive tests with consistent parameters, making large-scale experiments feasible. Regarding data analysis and interpretation, forensic software will assist in processing large datasets, applying ML for pattern recognition, and extracting relevant digital evidence efficiently. Visualization tools aid in identifying correlations and anomalies in forensic data, thereby enhancing insight generation.

For documentation and reporting, tools might generate standardized forensic reports, ensuring clarity, consistency, and compliance with legal requirements. Version control and data integrity tools are also essential to provide data and artifact provenance of experiment modifications, ensuring transparency and reproducibility. Regarding collaboration and dissemination, cloud-based platforms and collaborative tools enable researchers to share experimental results with the forensic community securely. Repositories, such as Zenodo or FigShare, and databases allow the storage and retrieval of forensic datasets, methodologies, and experimental results for future reference and validation.

By leveraging software tools, DF researchers can enhance the reliability, efficiency, and reproducibility of controlled experiments, ultimately strengthening the credibility of forensic science in legal and investigative contexts. For general concerns in controlled experimentation, DF still lacks certain types of tools that could enhance accuracy, reproducibility, and efficiency. While virtualized environments exist, there is a lack of standardized, widely accepted forensic testbed frameworks that can simulate real-world digital crimes with high fidelity. More realistic datasets reflecting modern cybercrime scenarios are needed to validate forensic tools under controlled conditions.

Current forensic tools primarily focus on analysis rather than simulating controlled experiments. Advanced tools that can generate realistic forensic cases, including synthetic yet representative evidence, are needed for testing forensic methodologies. Forensic tools often lack standardized benchmarking frameworks to validate their effectiveness under different conditions. There is a need for tools that can compare forensic methodologies against known datasets to measure accuracy, error rates, and the soundness of forensic conclusions. As AI is increasingly used in cybersecurity, DF experiment frameworks still lack AI-powered tools that can automate experiment design, assist in anomaly detection, and enhance evidence correlation.

Ensuring the integrity of forensic experiments is crucial, but there are limited tools to automatically track changes in DF datasets, log experiment modifications, and verify reproducibility. Blockchain-based DF experiment logging could improve transparency and auditability. With the growing diversity of platforms, cloud environments, and IoT devices, DF experimentation tools often fail to provide comprehensive cross-platform support. Therefore, more tools are needed to simulate and analyze DF cases involving hybrid environments (e.g., cloud, mobile, and embedded systems).

DF research lacks open, collaborative platforms where researchers can securely and ethically share, compare, and validate experimental results. Decentralized knowledge-sharing tools for DF methodologies might enhance reproducibility and collective learning. Addressing these gaps with advanced software tools would significantly improve the reliability, scalability, and credibility of DF-controlled experiments.

Striving for Openness

Open science and openness play a crucial role in enhancing controlled experimentation in DF, contributing significantly to the improvement of reproducibility, transparency, and scientific rigor in forensic investigations.

These principles enable a more rigorous and standardized approach to experimentation, fostering collaboration, knowledge sharing, and accountability. There exist several ways in which open science and openness can contribute to controlled experimentation in DF, as follows.

Open science and openness are essential for improving controlled experimentation in DF (Mombelli et al., 2024). They significantly enhance reproducibility, transparency, and scientific rigor in forensic investigations. By adopting these principles, researchers can employ a more standardized and rigorous approach to experimentation, which promotes collaboration, knowledge sharing, and accountability. Several ways in which open science and openness can support controlled experimentation in DF are as follows.

Enhancing Reproducibility in Digital Forensics

Reproducibility is crucial in DF (Horsman, 2024), as the reliability of findings can have significant legal consequences. Open science enhances reproducibility by making data, code, and methodologies publicly available. This allows other researchers to replicate experiments and validate results. By sharing datasets, forensic tools, and detailed procedures, the community can independently verify findings, thereby strengthening the credibility of forensic techniques and fostering trust in the field. This open approach can also help identify potential errors, biases, or limitations in forensic methods, ultimately leading to more robust and accurate results.

Promoting Transparency in Forensic Experimentation

Transparency in DF (Mombelli et al., 2024, Sunde and Franqueira, 2023) is crucial for ensuring that the methodologies and processes used in experiments are transparent, open to scrutiny, and accessible to the broader scientific community. Open science promotes the publication of detailed experimental designs, methods of data collection, and tools used in DF experiments. This openness enables others to evaluate the validity of the methods and ensures that experiments are conducted with scientific rigor. In DF, where decisions can significantly influence legal proceedings, transparency is essential to ensure that forensic processes are accurate and ethically sound.

Improving Data Sharing and Validation

One of the key principles of open science is the free and open sharing of research data (Allen et al., 2023, Breitinger and Jotterand, 2023). In the field of DF, this practice allows researchers to share large datasets used in forensic investigations. Other researchers can then utilize these datasets to validate results or test new forensic methodologies. Open access to forensic datasets ensures that researchers worldwide can apply the same data in their experiments, leading to more consistent and validated outcomes. Additionally, data sharing enables forensic practitioners to assess the effectiveness of tools and techniques under various conditions, ultimately enhancing the overall reliability of DF tools.

Leveraging Open-Source Tools for Scientific Rigor

Open-source software plays a crucial role in DF by ensuring that the forensic tools used are transparent and can be independently reviewed and modified by researchers (Huebner and Zanero, 2010). These tools are freely available to anyone in the forensic community, allowing users to examine the code, identify potential bugs, and confirm that the software performs reliably across various scenarios. This transparency enhances scientific rigor, ensuring that the tools used in forensic investigations are dependable, accurate, and free from proprietary limitations. Additionally, open-source tools facilitate collaborative improvements, enabling developers and researchers to work together to enhance the functionality of forensic software.

Standardizing Forensic Methods and Procedures

Open science can enhance the standardization of forensic methodologies by encouraging the publication of best practices, guidelines, and protocols. By making these resources accessible to the broader forensic community, researchers can develop and implement standardized procedures that ensure consistency and reliability in investigations. Standardization is especially crucial in DF, where maintaining the integrity of evidence throughout the investigative process is vital. Open science offers a platform for sharing and refining these standards, ensuring that forensic methods are widely accepted and scientifically valid.

Supporting Pre-Registration of Forensic Research Plans

Pre-registration (Lakens and Ditroilo, 2024; Chin et al., 2020) involves publicly declaring the research methods and hypotheses before experimentation. In the field of DF (Sijtsma et al., 2021), this practice can significantly reduce bias and ensure that experimental procedures are robust. By pre-registering their studies, researchers commit to following a transparent and predefined research plan. This helps prevent selective reporting of results and ensures that experiments are conducted rigorously. Pre-registration enhances the integrity of forensic research by holding researchers accountable for their initial study designs and protocols.

Ensuring Long-Term Archiving and Preservation of Research

The long-term preservation of research data and publications is crucial for the sustained development of DF (AlKhanafseh and Surakhi, 2024). Open science plays a vital role in this process by promoting the archiving of data, methodologies, and research outputs in publicly accessible repositories. This practice ensures that forensic data remains accessible for future generations of researchers, enabling them to build upon previous work and refine existing forensic methods. Additionally, long-term archiving guarantees that forensic techniques and tools are transparent and accessible for ongoing scrutiny and validation.

Artificial Intelligence and Machine Learning

AI and ML play a crucial role in enhancing the planning, execution, and sharing of controlled experiments in DF. Their integration helps manage the growing complexity and volume of digital data, thereby improving the accuracy and efficiency of forensic analyses.

During the planning phase of digital forensic experiments, AI plays a vital role in designing effective methodologies. It allows researchers to analyze large datasets to uncover patterns and anomalies (Padma and Don, 2022). This capability is essential for developing hypotheses and defining the scope of investigations. For example, the application of artificial neural networks in forensic science has shown promise in predicting future criminal activities by analyzing historical data, which can inform the strategic planning of forensic experiments. In controlled experiments, ML algorithms help automate the analysis of digital evidence, improving both the accuracy and speed of investigations. The application of data mining techniques in forensic tasks has been investigated to enhance the classification and interpretation of digital artifacts, thereby streamlining the investigative process (Tallón-Ballesteros and Riquelme, 2014).

The dissemination of findings from DF experiments is enhanced by AI, particularly through the automation of reporting and the generation of understandable results (Alam and Demir, 2024). Explainable AI models, such as those used for file type classification, provide transparency in the decision-making process. This transparency is crucial for the credibility and acceptance of forensic reports in legal contexts.

AI plays a crucial role in addressing challenges related to the realism and representativeness of data used in forensic experiments. Conversations about data realism emphasize the necessity for AI-driven methods to generate synthetic datasets that closely resemble real-world scenarios. This approach enhances the validity of experimental outcomes (Göbel et al., 2023). Additionally, AI aids in the standardization and optimization of forensic methodologies (Solanke and Biasiotti, 2022). Research aimed at assessing and refining AI techniques in DF highlights the need to establish standardized protocols to ensure consistency and reliability in DF experiments.

The use of AI in cybersecurity enhances DF efforts by enabling proactive threat detection and response (Apruzzese et al., 2023). A thorough understanding of ML's role in cybersecurity highlights its application in identifying vulnerabilities and mitigating potential threats, which is essential for DF investigations. The integration of AI and ML into DF greatly improves the planning, execution, and sharing of controlled experiments. By automating complex analyses, enhancing data management, and delivering predictive insights, these technologies make forensic investigations more efficient and effective, ultimately strengthening the overall cybersecurity infrastructure.

How to "Pedal to the Medal" in DF Experimentation?

To accelerate and enhance the rigor of controlled experimentation in DF, it is essential to adopt structured methodologies and adhere to established best practices. To do so, key strategies are presented.

Implement Formal Experimental Designs

Utilizing structured experimental frameworks ensures clarity and reproducibility in research. The Framework for Reliable Experimental Design (FRED) (Adel et al., 2024) offers a systematic approach to designing and conducting experiments in DF, emphasizing the importance of defining hypotheses, variables, and methodologies. In addition, as shown in Sections 3.1 and 3.2, ExperDF-CM and ExperDF-Onto are a straightforward advance in formalizing the design of DF experiments.

Adhere to Established Standards and Best Practices

Following international standards and best practice guidelines enhances the credibility of forensic investigations. Resources like the "Standards and Best Practices in Digital and Multimedia Forensics" provide comprehensive reviews of relevant standards, including those from ASTM International, and discuss best practices for laboratory accreditation and examiner certification (Li et al., 2015).

Emphasize Quality Assurance

Implementing quality assurance measures is crucial to ensure the reliability of forensic findings. Integrating advanced data validation techniques and maintaining stringent documentation practices can significantly enhance the accuracy and efficiency of investigations (Iftikhar et al., 2023).

Stay Abreast of Emerging Challenges and Innovations

The DF landscape is continually evolving with new technologies and associated challenges. Engaging with current literature, such as surveys on the industrial control system DF, can provide insights into recent advancements and future directions in the field (Cook et al., 2023).

By integrating these strategies, researchers and practitioners can enhance the efficiency, reliability, and credibility of controlled experiments in DF, thereby advancing the field and ensuring robust investigative outcomes.

Conclusion

This chapter has underscored the paramount importance of controlled experimentation in the field of DF. Experimentation serves as the bedrock for developing, validating, and refining the methodologies and tools essential for the accurate and legally defensible acquisition, examination, analysis, and reporting of digital evidence. As the digital landscape continues to evolve with the proliferation of cloud computing, IoT devices, and the integration of AI and NLP, the need for rigorous and well-documented experimental practices becomes increasingly critical to ensure the ongoing effectiveness and credibility of digital forensic investigations.

The chapter has also highlighted several significant challenges that currently impede the progress of controlled experimentation in DF. These include a lack of standardization and comprehensive documentation of experimental procedures, which hinders the reproducibility and reliability of research outcomes. The scarcity of realistic datasets, the absence of standardized forensic testbed frameworks, and the need for more advanced tools for controlled experiment simulation and benchmarking are further compounding issues. Addressing these shortcomings is crucial for strengthening the scientific foundation of the discipline.

To overcome these challenges and enhance the rigor of DF experimentation, the chapter has proposed several prospective actions. These include the development and adoption of support tooling to aid in all phases of experimentation, the embrace of open science principles to foster reproducibility and transparency, and the strategic integration of AI and ML to improve the efficiency and accuracy of experimental processes. Furthermore, the chapter emphasizes the importance of implementing formal experimental designs and adhering to established standards and best practices.

Ultimately, by actively addressing the identified challenges and embracing the proposed future actions, the DF community can significantly enhance the reliability, scalability, and credibility of controlled experiments. This, in turn, will lead to more robust investigative outcomes, strengthen the admissibility of digital evidence in legal proceedings, and ensure that the field remains at the forefront of combating digital crime in an increasingly complex technological world.

References

Adel, A., Ahsan, A., and Davison, C. (2024). Ethicore: Ethical compliance and oversight framework for digital forensic readiness. *Information,* 15(6).

Alam, S. and Demir, A. (2024). Sift: Sifting file types - application of explainable artificial intelligence in cyber forensics. *Cybersecurity,* 7(52).

AlKhanafseh, M. and Surakhi, O. (2024). Evidence preservation in digital forensics: An approach using blockchain and LSTM-based steganography. *Electronics,* 13(18).

Allen, C. I., Payne, S. H., and Valentine, J. L. (2023). Ethical data sharing in forensic research. *Forensic Science International: Synergy*, 6:100322.

Apruzzese, G., Laskov, P., Montes de Oca, E., Mallouli, W., Brdalo Rapa, L., Grammatopoulos, A. V., and Di Franco, F. (2023). The role of machine learning in cybersecurity. *Digital Threats*, 4(1).

Balon, T., Herlopian, K., Baggili, I., and Grajeda-Mendez, C. (2021). Forensic artifact finder (forensicaf): An approach & tool for leveraging crowd-sourced curated forensic artifacts. In *Proceedings of the 16th International Conference on Availability, Reliability and Security, ARES '21,* New York, NY, USA. Association for Computing Machinery.

Beebe, N. (2009). Digital forensic research: The good, the bad and the unaddressed. In Peterson, G. and Shenoi, S., editors, *Advances in Digital Forensics* V, pages 17–36, Berlin, Heidelberg. Springer Berlin Heidelberg.

Blancaflor, E., Arpilleda, J. A., Garcia, A. U., Monasterial, J. A., and Sulit, R. R. (2023). A literature review on the various trends of digital forensics usage in combating cybercrimes. In *Proceedings of the 2023 6th International Conference on Electronics, Communications and Control Engineering, ICECC* '23, page 132–138, New York, NY, USA. Association for Computing Machinery.

Breitinger, F. and Jotterand, A. (2023). Sharing datasets for digital forensic: A novel taxonomy and legal concerns. *Forensic Science International: Digital Investigation*, 45:301562.

Casino, F., Dasaklis, T. K., Spathoulas, G. P., Anagnostopoulos, M., Ghosal, A., Borocz, I., Solanas, A., Conti, M., and Patsakis, C. (2022). Research trends, challenges, and emerging topics in digital forensics: A review of reviews. *IEEE Access*, 10:25464–25493.

Chin, J. M., McFadden, R., and Edmond, G. (2020). Forensic science needs registered reports. *Forensic Science International: Synergy*, 2:41–45.

Cook, M., Marnerides, A., Johnson, C., and Pezaros, D. (2023). A survey on industrial control system digital forensics: Challenges, advances and future directions. *Commun. Surveys Tuts,* 25(3):1705–1747.

Costa, L., Barbosa, S., and Cunha, J. (2024). Evaluating tools for enhancing reproducibility in computational scientific experiments. In *Proceedings of the 2nd ACM Conference on Reproducibility and Replicability, ACM REP '24,* page 46–51, New York, NY, USA. Association for Computing Machinery.

Daniël Lakens, Cristian Mesquida, Sajedeh Rasti, and Ditroilo, M. (2024). The benefits of preregistration and registered reports. *Evidence-Based Toxicology*, 2(1):2376046.

Dunsin, D., Ghanem, M. C., Ouazzane, K., and Vassilev, V. (2024). A comprehensive analysis of the role of artificial intelligence and machine learning in modern digital forensics and incident response. *Forensic Science International: Digital Investigation,* 48:301675.

Göbel, T., Baier, H., and Breitinger, F. (2023). Data for digital forensics: Why a discussion on "how realistic is synthetic data" is dispensable. *Digital Threats*, 4(3).

Hassan, Z., Treude, C., Norrish, M., Williams, G., and Potanin, A. (2024). Reproducibility debt: Challenges and future pathways. In *Companion Proceedings of the 32nd ACM International Conference on the Foundations of Software Engineering, FSE 2024,* page 462–466, New York, NY, USA. Association for Computing Machinery.

Horsman, G. (2024). Sources of error in digital forensics. *Forensic Science International: Digital Investigation,* 48:301693.

Huebner, E. and Zanero, S. (2010). *Open Source Software for Digital Forensics.* Springer Publishing Company, Incorporated, 1st edition.

Iftikhar, A., Farooq, R., Mumtaz, M., Hussain, S., Akhtar, M., et al. (2023). Quality assurance in digital forensic investigations: Optimal strategies and emerging innovations. *Austin J Forensic Sci Criminol, 1*0(2).

John, J. L. (2012). Digital forensics and preservation. York: Digital Preservation Coalition. (Technology Watch Report 12-03).

Li, S., Dhami, M. K., and Ho, A. T. (2015). *Standards and Best Practices in Digital and Multimedia Forensics,* chapter 2, pages 38–93. John Wiley Sons, Ltd.

Martini, B. and Choo, K.-K. R. (2012). An integrated conceptual digital forensic framework for cloud computing. *Digital investigation,* 9(2):71–80.

Masud, M. Z., Hassan, A., Shah, W. M., Abdul-Latip, S. F., Ahmad, R., Ariffin, A., and Yunos, Z. (2021). A review of digital forensics framework for blockchain in cryptocurrency technology. In *2021 3rd International Cyber Resilience Conference (CRC),* pages 1–6.

Mir, S. S., Shoaib, U., and Sarfraz, M. S. (2016). Analysis of digital forensic investigation models. *Int. J. Comput. Sci. Inform. Secur*, 14(11).

Mombelli, S., Lyle, J. R., and Breitinger, F. (2024). Fairness in digital forensics datasets' metadata – and how to improve it. *Forensic Science International: Digital Investigation,* 48:301681. DFRWS EU 2024 - Selected Papers from the 11th Annual Digital Forensics Research Conference Europe.

OliveiraJr, E., Silva, T. J., Zorzo, A. F., and Neu, C. V. (2022). Digital forensics experimentation: *Analysis and recommendations. Forensic Sci Rev*, 34(1):21–41.

OliveiraJr, E., Zorzo, A. F., and Neu, C. V. (2020). Towards a conceptual model for promoting digital forensics experiments. *Forensic Science International: Digital Investigation,* 35:301014.

OliveiraJr, E., Zorzo, A. F., and Neu, C. V. (2021). Experimentation of digital multimedia forensics: State of the art and research gaps. *WIREs Forensic Science,* 3(4):e1405.

Padma, K. and Don, K. (2022). *Artificial Neural Network Applications in Analysis of Forensic Science In Cyber Security and Digital Forensics (eds M.M. Ghonge, S. Pramanik, R. Mangrulkar and D.-N. Le),* pages 59–72, Wiley.

Palmer, G. (2001). Dfrws technical report: A road map for digital forensic research. In *Digital forensic research workshop*, volume 42.

Raghavan, S. (2013). Digital forensic research: current state of the art. *Csi Transactions on ICT,* 1:91–114.

Salem, Y., Owda, M., and Owda, A. Y. (2023). A comprehensive review of digital forensics frameworks for internet of things (IoT) devices. In *2023 International Conference on Information Technology (ICIT),* pages 89–96.

Sijtsma, K., Emons, W. H. M., Steneck, N. H., and Bouter, L. M. (2021). Steps toward preregistration of research on research integrity. *Res Integr Peer Rev*, 6(5).

Silva, T. J., Mazur, A. H., OliveiraJr, E., Zorzo, A. F., and Barcellos, M. P. (2025). An ontology for promoting controlled experimentation in digital forensics. *Forensic Science International: Digital Investigation,* 52:301845.

Solanke, A. A. and Biasiotti, M. A. (2022). Digital forensics AI: Evaluating, standardizing and optimizing digital evidence mining techniques. *Ku¨nstl Intell*, 36:143–161.

Sunde, N. and Franqueira, V. N. (2023). Adding transparency to uncertainty: An argument-based method for evaluative opinions. *Forensic Science International: Digital Investigation*, 47:301657.

Tallón-Ballesteros, A. J. and Riquelme, J. C. (2014). *Data Mining Methods Applied to a Digital Forensics Task for Supervised Machine learning,* pages 413–428. Springer International Publishing, Cham.

Tiwari, A., Mehrotra, V., Goel, S., Naman, K., Maurya, S., and Agarwal, R. (2021). Developing trends and challenges of digital forensics. In *2021 5th International Conference on Information Systems and Computer Networks (ISCON),* pages 1–5.

Ukwen, D. O. and Karabatak, M. (2021). Review of NLP-based systems in digital forensics and cybersecurity. In *2021 9th International Symposium on Digital Forensics and Security (ISDFS),* pages 1–9.

Wohlin, C., Runeson, P., Hst, M., Ohlsson, M. C., Regnell, B., and Wessln, A. (2012). *Experimentation in Software Engineering.* Springer Publishing Company, Incorporated.

Wu, C., Chakravorti, T., Carroll, J. M., and Rajtmajer, S. (2024). Integrating measures of replicability into scholarly search: Challenges and opportunities. In *Proceedings of the 2024 CHI Conference on Human Factors in Computing Systems, CHI'24,* New York, NY, USA. Association for Computing Machinery.

Chapter 2

Advancements in Forensic Science Using AI and Deep Learning

Md Al Amin Tokder*

Computer Science and Engineering, Rajshahi University of Engineering and Technology, Rajshahi, Bangladesh

Abstract

Bloodstain detection is crucial in Crime Scene Investigation (CSI), as it provides valuable insights into the events that transpired, aids in identifying individuals involved, and supports the investigative process in criminal cases. It helps investigators understand what happened, who was involved, and when it occurred. Advancements in forensic science, particularly bloodstain analysis, have become imperative for enhancing crime scene reconstruction. Conventional methods, such as Deoxyribonucleic Acid (DNA) profiling and other chemical analysis methods, often take more time to identify a bloodstain. Instead of DNA profiling, this chapter contributes to the advancement of forensic science by introducing an innovative approach to bloodstain identification and classification by using a 3-Dimensional Convolutional Neural Network (3D CNN) model utilizing the capabilities of Hyperspectral Imaging (HIS). Here, we introduce an optimized 3D CNN with the Mish activation function and find the optimal accuracy. This work will help facilitate faster investigations of crime scenes and the analysis of forensic cases. The optimized 3D CNN model was applied, resulting in performance that outperformed the existing CNN model. An accuracy of 97% was achieved, surpassing the existing 3D CNN (95%) and hybrid

---

* Corresponding Author's Email: alamintokdercse@gmail.com

In: Frontiers of Forensic Science: Innovation, Technology, and Justice
Editor: Walid M. Khalilia
ISBN: 979-8-90134-160-5

CNN (96%) models. Furthermore, the number of parameters was reduced from 291,895 to 125,943.

Keywords: blood stain analysis, optimized 3D-CNN, forensic science, crime scene investigation, hyperspectral image, principal component analysis

Introduction

In Dynamic criminal investigation, the field of forensic science plays a pivotal role in collecting, detecting, and analyzing evidence to facilitate successful case resolution. The examination of body fluids, particularly bloodstains, holds significant importance during violent crime scenes as an integral aspect of forensic science (De Vittori, et al., 2016; Liu, et al., 2017; Rosenblatt, et al., 2019; Książek, et al., 2020). The presence of blood at such scenes makes it a valuable form of forensic evidence, presenting both challenges and opportunities for thorough analysis. Collecting, detecting, and analyzing evidence from a crime scene is highly challenging for a successful and active criminal investigation (Wu, et al., 2020).

Body fluids are considered a crucial asset in forensic inquiries, especially in violent crime scenes. Among these, blood holds the highest importance in forensic analysis (Hurley, et al., 2009). Identifying bloodstains and determining their age are crucial for solving a crime. By examining the Blood Stain Pattern (BSP), we can gain insight into what happened during the crime and potentially identify those involved. Estimating the age of bloodstains helps us piece together the timeline of events, which is essential for finding suspects (de Bruin, et al., 2011). Our primary goal is to develop a method for definitively verifying that a stain is indeed composed of blood.

Visually, bloodstains are similar to other substances in color and appearance. This similarity complicates the differentiation process. Identifying genuine bloodstains for DNA testing is crucial in forensic investigations to avoid wasting time and resources on false positives, such as stains that may appear brown or similar to blood but are not actually blood. Dried bloodstains undergo various transformations as they age, resulting in alterations in color and texture. The identification of dried blood has emerged as a significant challenge in forensic science (Butt et al., 2022). The spectral components of blood can be used to estimate the depth of a wound.

The main key component of blood is hemoglobin, which is a derivative of hemoglobin, namely Met hemoglobin (metHb) and Oxyhemoglobin (oxyHb).

The distinctive spectral peaks of metHb and oxyHb in the Visible Light Spectrum (VIS) enable their identification and differentiation from other substances (Gautam, et al., 2020). It is crucial to understand how these entities behave when confronted with images that exhibit variations in both spatial and spectral features. For our work, we use a publicly available Hyperspectral Imaging (HSI). Dataset that ensures transparency and accessibility (Romaszewski, et al., 2021). Due to the HSI dataset's characteristics of having high spectral but low spatial information, conventional 1-Dimensional (1D) and 2-Dimensional (2D) Convolutional Neural Networks (CNNs) are not suitable for this task. These networks would only handle spectral data, neglecting spatial information. To overcome this limitation, a 3D CNN is more appropriate. These models process data across three dimensions concurrently, allowing for effective learning of hierarchical features. This approach needs fewer parameters than 1D and 2D CNNs and minimizes information loss.

Related Work

HSI is a novel imaging technique gaining momentum in the medical realm, especially for disease diagnosis and providing visual guidance during surgical procedures (Al-Sarayreh et al., 2018). HSI is a method used in forensic science because it is quick, does not cause any damage, and does not require physical contact with the evidence (Fonseca, et al., 2022).

Forensic labs employ various approaches to identify bloodstains. Presumptive tests are initial assessments that provide an indication but may not confirm definitively. The Kastle-Meyer (KM) test is specifically highlighted as one of the presumptive tests employed in forensic labs. The specificity of the KM reaction compared to Benzedrine in identifying stains from various sources, such as bodily fluids, fruits, vegetables, and chemicals. The KM reaction exhibits higher specificity in contrast to Benzedrine (Zulfiqar, et al., 2021). Besides, Luminol is highly regarded and widely recognized as one of the most significant assays (tests or analyses) in forensic science. Luminol's effectiveness can be influenced by environmental conditions, such as ambient light, humidity, and temperature, which can impact the sensitivity and reliability of the test. This work compares different luminol formulations, focusing on their luminescence and longevity (Taylor et al., 2023).

Advancements in laser technology and light detectors have significantly enhanced spectroscopic methods for characterizing molecules. These improvements have opened new opportunities for on-site, conclusive identification of body fluids at crime scenes (Zapata Arr′aez, et al., 2015). In a previous study conducted by Zulfiqar et al. (2021), reflectance spectra from 35 non-blood stains and 40 bloodstains, all of which were on white cotton fabric, were analyzed. All the models tested demonstrated the ability to accurately identify deposited stains as blood, with a maximum accuracy of 94% and a minimum accuracy of 81%. The analysis yielded a correct classification rate of 92% during a Leave-One-Out Cross-Validation (LOOCV) process, where each spectrum was temporarily excluded from the model's training set and then tested against the model (Mistek et al., 2019; Fonseca et al., 2022).

The identification of blood traces is facilitated by non-contact techniques, primarily due to challenges in maintaining temperature and humidity with traditional methods. Researchers turned to HSI because it enables blood identification without contact, thereby reducing the risk of contamination and destruction. The advantages include rapid data collection, eliminating the need for sample preparation, and reducing the workload in laboratories (Hart et al., 2022).

The current methods for detecting and identifying bloodstains, which involve visual examination and presumptive tests, have limitations, including false positives and potential interference with DNA tests. They introduced a new way of using HSI, specifically in the visible wavelength range, to detect and confirm blood stains on different colored surfaces without touching or damaging them. The method is capable of distinguishing between bloodstains and nine other red-colored substances, as well as identifying blood in approximately 40 reddish stains (Cadd et al., 2018).

Previous research conducted by Ullah et al. (2024) introduced an Active Learning (AL) pipeline designed to address the challenge of sample selection in HSI classification. They utilized deep convolution networks with a hybrid dilated residual approach, aiming to improve HSI classification performance by adaptively selecting spectral bands and overcoming limitations associated with manually crafted selections.

In a previous study conducted by Kaul and Raina (2022), the robustness of HSI classification was improved by investigating the application of Deep Support Vector Machine (DSVM) with various kernel functions. The challenge of stain detection is particularly in confirming whether, in a crime scene, a stain is a bloodstain or not. To overcome this difficulty, confirming bloodstains is challenging, especially considering the implications of false positives. DNA analysis is a powerful method for identifying suspects;

however, this approach is costly and time-consuming. Consequently, if a false positive occurs, such as with a stain that appears similar to blood but is not, it wastes not only significant time but also resources. Therefore, it is essential to develop accurate and efficient methods for confirming bloodstains at crime scenes to avoid potential false positives and the associated costs and resources.

Dataset

HSI contains both spatial and spectral information. For the detection and classification of blood, HSI can detect different forms of hemoglobin. The dataset contains various types of materials, including blood (1), blood-like components such as poster paint (5), ketchup (2), acrylic paint (7), beetroot juice, artificial blood (3), and uncertain blood, tomato concentrate (6), shown in Figure 1 and Figure 2.

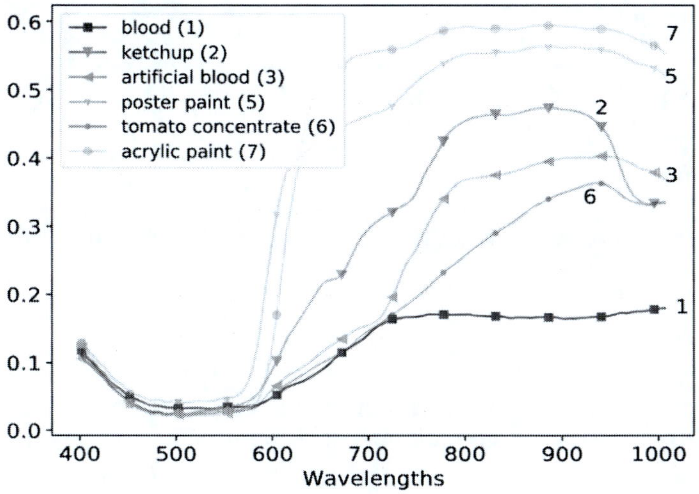

Source: Authors

Figure 1. HSI dataset for different types of materials at different wavelengths.

Over the span of three weeks, an array of images was captured, each possessing its unique ambiance crafted by varying backgrounds and intensities of illuminating light. The photos were captured over three weeks and vary in terms of background composition and lighting intensity. This dataset has 14 HSIs, which are in ENVI format. The images contain blood and similar substances like tomato concentrate (6), artificial blood (3), and acrylic paint (7) (Figure 2). Over the span of three weeks, an array of images was captured, each possessing its unique ambiance crafted by varying backgrounds and intensities of illuminating light. Substances present in the dataset are 519 × 696 pixels (each pixel contains 113 bands).

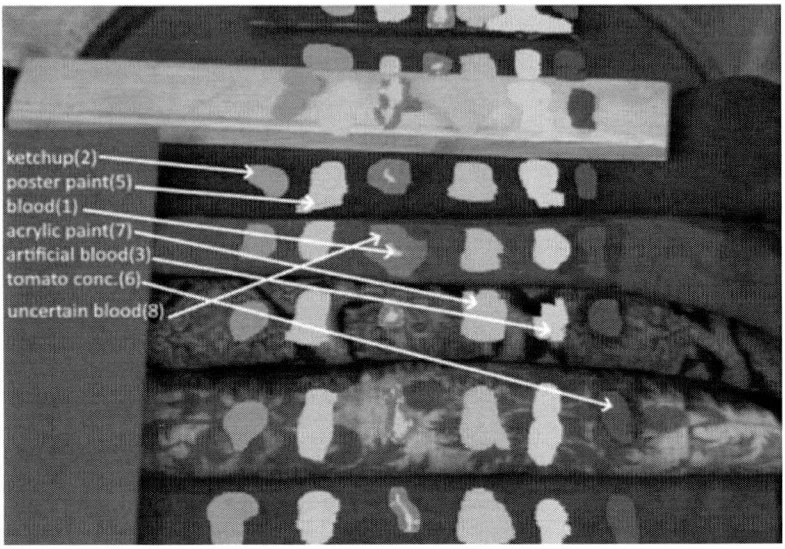

Source: Authors

Figure 2. An array of images for different types of materials using HIS.

Methodology

HSI data is akin to a 3D cube, where each point represents a pixel in an image. It contains information about both the color and location of each pixel. This cube is made up of width, height, and depth, where depth represents the number of different colors or spectral bands captured in the image. Each pixel is labeled with a vector indicating its category, with similarities and differences existing within each category. The image may contain overlapping categories, making it challenging to distinguish them accurately Figure 3.

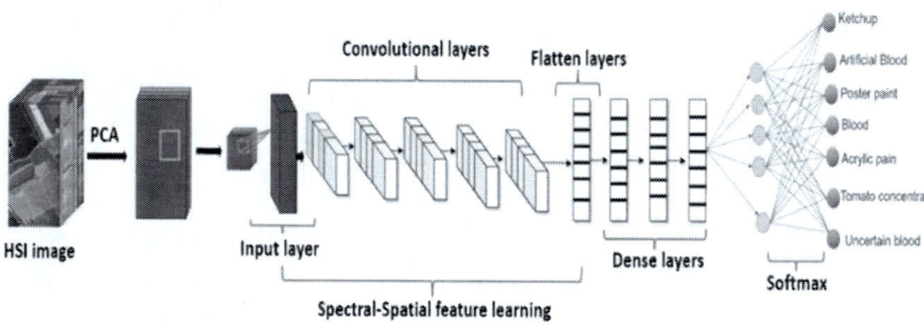

Figure 3. Proposed architecture of 3D CNN (Kernel size= 3x3x7; 3D $_{input}$= 9.9.15.1).

To simplify this complex data, preprocessing is performed using Principal Component Analysis (PCA), which reduces the number of colors while preserving crucial spatial information, thereby facilitating analysis and interpretation. To effectively process HSI data for image classification, a 3D CNN is employed, utilizing its unique structure tailored for analyzing spatial-spectral information. Firstly, the HSI cube is divided into small, overlapping 3D patches to analyze individual pixels closely. These patches enable localized analysis centered on individual pixels. These patches are then fed into the 3D CNN, which comprises multiple layers of 3D convolutional operations. Unlike traditional 2D CNNs, which analyze spatial information only, 3D CNNs operate on both spatial and spectral dimensions simultaneously, enabling them to capture the complex spatial-spectral patterns inherent in HSI data. The structure of the 3D CNN comprises multiple layers of 3D convolutional kernels, followed by activation functions that introduce nonlinearity. In this image classification algorithm, the process begins by dissecting the HSI cube into smaller, overlapping 3D patches. These patches are meticulously crafted, with their truth labels discerned based on the central pixel's label. Following this initial step, neighbor patches Np ∈ Rw×w×B are crafted, employing a spatial window of w × w centered on specific spatial coordinates (x, y). Each of these neighbors' patches, denoted as n patches, covers a designated area, spanning the width and height dimensions of the HSI cube.

This coverage ranges from (x − w + 1/2) to (x + w − 1/2) and (y − w + 1/2) to (y + w − 1/2). In 3D CNN, 3D convolutional procedures and 3D kernel extracts spatial and spectral information from HSI cube.

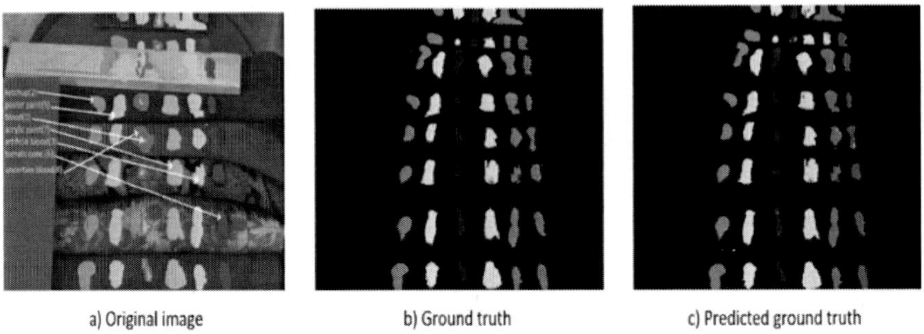

Figure 4. Original image (a), ground truth (b), and predicted ground truth after 3D CNN (c).

Instead of the commonly used ReLU function, the Mish activation function is used here to enhance feature extraction and learning capabilities. This function introduces smoothness and better gradients compared to the ReLU function, thereby improving the learning process. The 3D CNN architecture, augmented with the Mish activation function, effectively processes HSI data, extracting discriminative spatial-spectral features crucial for accurate image classification tasks (Figure 4). The Mish activation function is defined as:

$$f(x) = x \cdot \tanh(\ln(1 + ex)) \tag{1}$$

Where: x: Represents the input value at each position in the 3x3 matrix; tanh (): The hyperbolic tangent function, which maps values to the range of (-1, 1); ln (): The natural logarithm function; 1 + ex: An exponential term added to 1 (Srivastava et al., 2023). 3 × 3 kernel size is used.

Table 1 shows other details. The proposed model contains 125943 trainable parameters. Adam optimizer is used for optimizing the Softmax function. For training and validating the 3D CNN model, 10 epochs are used (Reyad et al., 2023).

Table 1. Model details

Layer (type)	Output Shape	Param #
input_1 (InputLayer)	(None, 9, 9, 15, 1)	0
conv3d_1 (Conv3D)	(None, 7, 7, 9, 8)	512
conv3d_2 (Conv3D)	(None, 5, 5, 5, 16)	5776
conv3d_3 (Conv3D)	(None, 3, 3, 3, 32)	13856
conv3d_4 (Conv3D)	(None, 1, 1, 1, 64)	55360
flatten_1 (Flatten)	(None, 64)	0
dense_1 (Dense)	(None, 256)	16640
dense_2 (Dense)	(None, 128)	32896
dense_3 (Dense)	(None, 7)	903
Total params: 125943 (491.96 KB)		
Trainable params: 125943 (491.96 KB)		
Non-trainable params: 0 (0.00 Byte)		

Experimental Setup

This dataset is available online (www.kaggle.com) and was experimented with on the online platform Kaggle.com. Kaggle provides free access to NVIDIA TESLA P100 GPUs. Kaggle offers a generous allocation of cold storage, providing users with 358.27 GB of storage space. Additionally, Kaggle generously allocates a substantial amount of Random Access Memory (RAM), providing users with 25 GB of memory to efficiently handle large datasets and complex computational tasks. This experiment is divided into three separate sets (Train/Validation/Test). These sets are Training (1690, 9, 9, 15, 1), Validation (1690, 9, 9, 15, 1), and Test (30424, 9, 9, 15, 1). The whole dataset is split into three ratios. Here Training: Validation: Test were 5%: 5%: 90% respectively.

Classification Result

The 15 most informative bands are selected by using the PCA method. While training the model, a learning rate of 0.001 is used. In comparison, the proposed 3D CNN model's Overall Accuracy (OA) is higher than that of the traditional 3D CNN model. Before optimizing, the CNN model used the traditional ReLU activation function. After optimizing the 3D CNN model, the Mish activation function was employed, and the softmax function was utilized in the output layers. The whole evaluation result is shown in Tables 2 and 3.

The overall accuracy increases from 95% to 97%, as shown in Figure 6. For this experiment, the whole dataset is divided into three separate sets. For training purposes, 5% is used, 5% is used for validation purposes, and 90% is considered the test set. In this experiment, Mish's function performs well, as it is a non-monotonic function that possesses self-regularization properties and avoids the vanishing gradient problem, making it superior to ReLU activation functions.

Table 2. Classifier performance

Classifier	Accuracy	Macro (avg.)	Weight (avg.)	Parameter
3D CNN	0.95	0.95	0.95	291895
Hybrid CNN	0.96	0.97	0.96	291895
Proposed 3D CNN	0.97	0.96	0.97	125943

Table 3. Proposed 3D CNN model results for the used materials

Class	Precision	Recall	F1-Score	Support
blood	0.99	0.96	0.97	2668
ketchup	1.00	0.98	0.99	5259
artificial blood	0.93	0.92	0.93	5774
poster paint	1.00	1.00	1.00	5963
tomato concentrate	0.89	0.93	0.91	3541
acrylic paint	0.98	0.98	0.98	7219

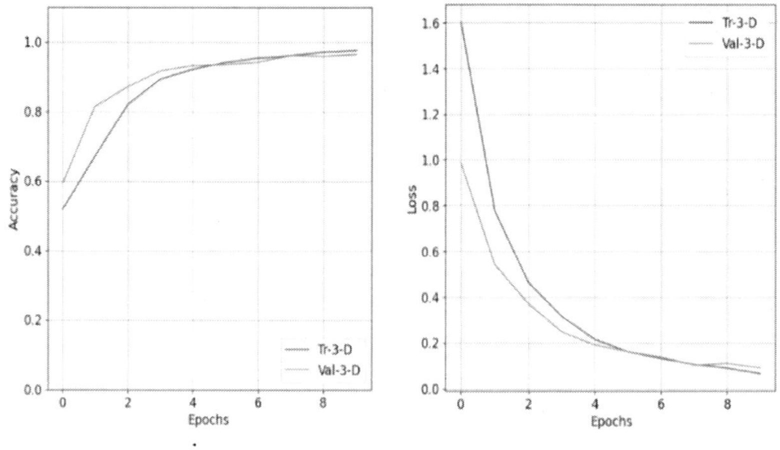

Figure 5. Learning curve of optimized 3D CNN.

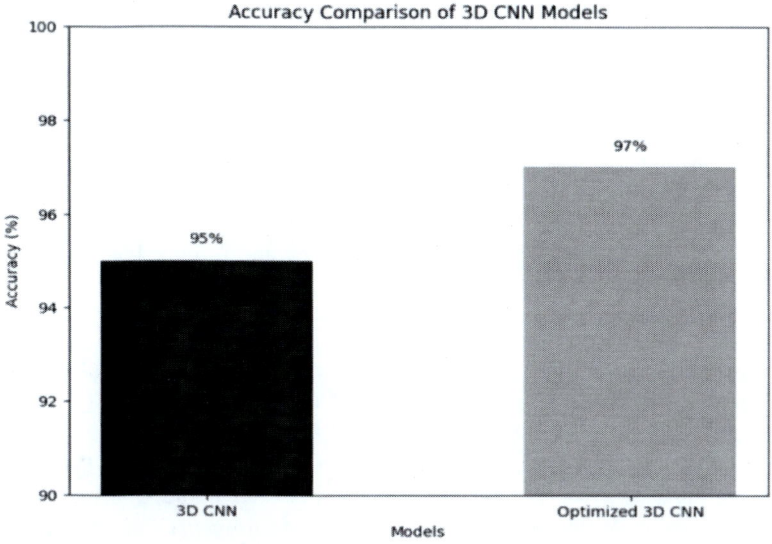

Figure 6. Comparison of overall accuracy for 3D CNN and optimized 3D CNN models.

Conclusion

The proposed 3D CNN model, optimized using the Mish activation function and PCA-based band selection, outperforms the traditional 3D CNN model by increasing overall accuracy from 95% to 97%. The use of Mish activation, due to its non-monotonic and self-regularizing properties, proves more effective than ReLU.

References

Al-Sarayreh, M., M. Reis, M., Qi Yan, W., & Klette, R. (2018). Detection of Red-Meat Adulteration by Deep Spectral–Spatial Features in Hyperspectral Images. *Journal of Imaging*, *4*(5), 63. https://doi.org/10.3390/jimaging4050063.

Butt, M. H. F., Ayaz, H., Ahmad, M., Li, J. P., and Kuleev, R. (2022). A fast and compact hybrid CNN for hyperspectral imaging-based bloodstain classification. *IEEE Congress on Evolutionary Computation (CEC),* pp. 1–8, IEEE, 2022. https://doi.org/10.1109/CEC55065.2022.9870277.

Cadd, S., Li, B., Beveridge, P., O'Hare, W. T., & Islam, M. (2018). Age Determination of Blood-Stained Fingerprints Using Visible Wavelength Reflectance Hyperspectral Imaging. *Journal of Imaging*, *4*(12), 141. https://doi.org/10.3390/jimaging4120141.

de Bruin, K. G., Stoel, R. D., & Limborgh, J. C. (2011). Improving the point of origin determination in bloodstain pattern analysis. *Journal of forensic sciences*, *56*(6), 1476–1482. https://doi.org/10.1111/j.1556-4029.2011.01841.x.

De Vittori, E., Barni, F., Lewis, S., Antonini, G., Rapone, C., Berti, A. (2016). Forensic application of a rapid one-step tetramethylbenzidine-based test for the presumptive trace detection of bloodstains at the crime scene and in the laboratory. *Forensic Chemistry, 2*, pp. 63-74. https://doi.org/10.1016/j.forc.2016.10.002.

Fonseca, A. C. S., Pereira, J. F. Q., Honorato, R. S., Bro, R., & Pimentel, M. F. (2022). Hierarchical classification models and Handheld NIR spectrometer to human bloodstains identification on different floor tiles. *Spectrochimica acta. Part A, Molecular and biomolecular spectroscopy*, *267*(Pt1), 120533. https://doi.org/10.1016/j.saa.2021.120533.

Gautam, R., Peoples, D., Jansen, K., O'Connor, M., Thomas, G., Vanga, S., Pence, I. J., & Mahadevan-Jansen, A. (2020). Feature Selection and Rapid Characterization of Bloodstains on Different Substrates. *Applied spectroscopy*, *74*(10), 1238–1251. https://doi.org/10.1177/0003702820937776.

Hart, A. J., Barnes, G. C., Fuller, F., Cornwell, A. M., Gyula, J., and Marsh, N. P. (2022). Finding blood in the dark: A comparison of infrared imaging devices for the detection of bloodstains on dark fabrics based on their resolution. *Forensic Science International, 330*, 111124. https://doi.org/10.1016/j.forsciint.2021.111124.

Hurley, I. P., Cook, R., Laughton, C. W., Pickles, N. A., Ireland, H. E., Williams, J. H. (2009). Detection of human blood by immunoassay for applications in forensic analysis. *Forensic Sci Int.*, 190(1-3):91-7. https://doi.org/10.1016/j.forsciint.2009.05.018.

Kaul, A., and Raina, S. (2022). Support vector machine versus convolutional neural network for hyperspectral image classification: A systematic review. *Concurrency Computat Pract Exper*. *34*(15):e6945. https://doi.org/10.1002/cpe.6945.

Książek, K., Romaszewski, M., Głomb, P., Grabowski, B., & Cholewa, M. (2020). Blood Stain Classification with Hyperspectral Imaging and Deep Neural Networks. *Sensors*, *20*(22), 6666. https://doi.org/10.3390/s20226666.

Liu, X., Sun, Q., Liu, B., Huang, B., and Fu, M. (2017). Hyperspectral image classification based on convolutional neural network and dimension reduction. *Chinese automation congress (CAC)*, pp. 1686–1690, *IEEE*, 2017.

Mistek, E., Halámková, L., and Lednev, I. K. (2019). Phenotype profiling for forensic purposes: Nondestructive potentially on scene attenuated total reflection fourier transform-infrared (atr ft-ir) spectroscopy of bloodstains. *Forensic Chemistry, 16*, 100176. https://doi.org/10.1016/j.forc.2019.100176.

Reyad, M., Sarhan, A. & Arafa, M. (2023). A modified Adam algorithm for deep neural network optimization. *Neural Comput & Applic* 35, 17095–17112. https://doi.org/10.1007/s00521-023-08568-z.

Romaszewski, M., Głomb, P., Sochan, A., and Cholewa, M. (2021). A dataset for evaluating blood detection in hyperspectral images. *Forensic science international,* 320, 110701. https://doi.org/10.48550/arXiv.2008.10254.

Rosenblatt, R., Halámková, L., Doty, K. C., de OliveiraJr, E. A., and Lednev, I. K. (2019). Raman spectroscopy for forensic bloodstain identification: method validation vs. environmental interferences. *Forensic Chemistry, 16:* 100175, 2019. https://doi.org/10.1016/j.forc.2019.100175.

Srivastava, V., Mishra, S., Gupta, N. (2023). Automatic Detection and Categorization of Road Traffic Signs using a Knowledge-Assisted Method, Procedia Computer Science, 218, 1280-1287. https://doi.org/10.1016/j.procs.2023.01.106.

Taylor, A., van Oorschot, R. A. H., & Durdle, A. (2023). Detection of fresh blood by luminol and DNA after walking over various substrates. *Australian Journal of Forensic Sciences, 56*(4), 432–441. https://doi.org/10.1080/00450618.2023.2195208.

Ullah, F., Ullah, I., Khan, R. U., Khan, S., Khan, K., and Pau, G. (2024). Conventional to Deep Ensemble Methods for Hyperspectral Image Classification: A Comprehensive Survey. *IEEE Journal of Selected Topics in Applied Earth Observations and Remote Sensing*, *17,* 3878-3916, 2024, https://doi.org/10.1109/JSTARS.2024.3353551.

Wu, T., Breitinger, F., and O'Shaughnessy, S. (2020). Digital forensic tools: Recent advances and enhancing the status quo. *Forensic Science International: Digital Investigation, 34*: 300999. https://doi.org/10.1016/j.fsidi.2020.300999.

Zapata Arráez, F., Fernández de la Ossa, M. d. l., García Ruiz, C. (2015). Emerging spectrometric techniques for the forensic analysis of body fluids. TrAC *Trends in Analytical Chemistry, 64,* 53-63. https://doi.org/10.1016/j.trac.2014.08.011.

Zulfiqar, M., Ahmad, M., Sohaib, A., Mazzara, M., & Distefano, S. (2021). Hyperspectral Imaging for Bloodstain Identification. *Sensors*, *21*(9), 3045. https://doi.org/10.3390/s21093045.

Chapter 3

The Criminal Liability of AI Crimes

Mohamed Said Zenati[1,*]
and Atailia Chaima[2]

[1]Laboratory for International Legal Changes and Their Impact on Algerian Legislation, Faculty of Law and Political Science, University of Echahid Hamma Lakhder , El Oued, Algeria
[2]Investment and Sustainable Development Laboratory, Faculty of Law and Political Science, University of Mohamed Ben Ahmed Oran 2, Oran, Algeria

Abstract

Modern technology has led to the widespread adoption of Artificial Intelligence (AI) technologies and their increasing reliance on them to handle various business and personal matters. This has led to several legal issues, especially regarding the criminal liability of these intelligent entities, as this liability is regarded as one of the legal consequences of a crime, an event recognized by law, meaning that the criminal bears the punishment set forth by the law. The widespread use of AI is causing an increase in crimes, necessitating a study of the legal challenges faced by legislators and judicial authorities in regulating its use and establishing a framework to protect people's lives and rights, with responsibility for identifying perpetrators and applying criminal penalties. The study investigates the criminal liability of AI entities, examining the extent to which criminal liability rules apply to crimes committed by AI. It employs a descriptive and analytical approach to clarify the concept of AI and link its use to legal texts. This study examines the nature of AI, its advantages and disadvantages, and the ongoing debate on criminal liability arising from AI-related crimes, with a focus on the continuing debate between supporters and opponents.

---

* Corresponding Author's Email: mohamedsaid-zenati@univ-eloued.dz

In: Frontiers of Forensic Science: Innovation, Technology, and Justice
Editor: Walid M. Khalilia
ISBN: 979-8-90134-160-5

Keywords: criminal liability, legal personality, artificial intelligence, penalties

Introduction

The use of Artificial Intelligence (AI) techniques and reliance on it in the conduct of all business and life matters has become a reality imposed by modern technology. This has raised numerous legal issues, particularly concerning the criminal liability of these intelligent entities, given that this liability is one of the legal consequences of the crime, a fact recognized by law, which results in the perpetrator of the crime being held accountable for the penalty established by legal rules.

AI in our current era is one of the most sensitive topics of great importance, due to its significant position. We do not find a field that does not utilize AI applications, so with this widespread use, crimes related to it will likely increase. Therefore, it was necessary to study this topic in terms of the legal challenges faced by legislators and judicial authorities, by regulating the use of these, and establishing a legal framework that ensures the sanctity of the lives and rights of people within society is not violated. In addition to determining the real perpetrator to whom the criminal penalty should be applied, it is necessary to identify the correct individual. The study aims to determine the criminal liability of AI entities by addressing the following question: To what extent do the rules of criminal liability apply to crimes committed by AI? Is the latter not culpable due to its lack of legal personality, or can it be held accountable as an original offender of the crime?

To answer this question, we adopted a descriptive approach in this study to clarify the concept of AI and an analytical approach to analyze the liability arising from the use of AI entities, aiming to link it to the legal texts that regulate or criminalize their use. To study this topic, we have divided this chapter into two main sections. The first section introduces the concept of AI, explaining what it is and its advantages and disadvantages. The second section addresses the criminal liability arising from AI crimes, examining the existing debate on establishing criminal liability between supporters and opponents, as well as the liability arising from crimes committed by AI entities.

The Legal Framework for Artificial Intelligence (AI)

AI is a science that focuses on creating machines that perform actions considered intelligent by humans. Despite the widespread application of AI technologies across all sectors and their rapid and limitless development, there remains ambiguity regarding the concept of AI entities. Accordingly, we have divided this section into two subsections: the first will address the idea of AI, and the second will discuss the advantages and disadvantages of AI in the criminal field.

The Concept of Artificial Intelligence (AI)

AI plays a vital role in various fields of life, including the criminal justice field, where different types of crimes are investigated and combated, prompting us to reexamine the definition of AI.

To know what AI is, it is necessary first to identify the concept of human intelligence. Which is defined as "the ability and skill to develop and find solutions to problems using codes, different research methods for problems, and the ability to use the acquired experience in deriving new information and knowledge, leading to the development of solutions to problems in a specific field." (Al-Najjar, 2010). The level of intelligence varies from one person to another. Human intelligence is responsible for the development and creativity in the growth of different civilizations. Given the importance of human intelligence, humans have always been and continue to search for the nature of intelligence and how to develop it.

Therefore, in this subsection, we address the definition of AI in language, followed by its definition in terminology.

I. Linguistic definition of AI: Intelligence means quick wit (Ibn Zakariya, 1979), and the word artificial means to make, and artificiality is an exaggeration of the gift, dignity, and favor (Abu al-Fadl, 1968). As for artificiality in the sense of exaggeration in making, and so-and-so made for himself: He chose it: What is learned by learning from the masters of industries, and what is not natural, and it is said industrial silk, i.e., the industrial source. A closer look at the words' industrial' or 'artificial' reveals that they are related to the act of making. This symbolizes the creation of something that is not natural, which is why this word encompasses all things that result from the manufacture and formation of things, distinguishing them from those that already exist and are born naturally without human intervention (Yassin, 2012). In fact, the word "artificial" shares with the word "intelligence" the characteristic of often being a compound word, and it is also a common word, as its meaning varies according to the compound word, such as artificial limbs, artificial memory, artificial nervous system, and others.

II. AI Scientific definition: Scientists for AI develop many definitions, but reaching a comprehensive definition has not yet been achieved, as most definitions are either based on technology and the purpose of AI as an application or a machine, while some choose to define it by looking at its characteristics that approach human intelligence.

John McCarthy, the godfather of AI (McCarthy, (n.d)), defined it as: "A means of creating a computer, a computer-controlled robot, or a program that thinks intelligently in the same way as intelligent humans; AI is achieved by studying how the human brain thinks, how humans learn, decide and act while trying to solve an issue, and then using the results of these as a basis for developing intelligent programs and systems." (Dahshan, 2020). AI can also be defined as 'A branch of computer science concerned with how machines can mimic human behavior. It is the science of creating computer devices and programs that can think like the human brain, learn as we learn, make decisions as we decide, and behave as we behave (Ibrahim, 2020). Additionally, it has been defined as: that branch of computer science through which computer programs can be created and designed to mimic human intelligence so that computers can perform specific tasks instead of humans, which require thinking, understanding, hearing, speaking, and moving in a logical and organized manner (Ibrahim, 2020). On the other hand, others have defined it as 'the simulation of human intelligence and understanding of its nature through the creation of computer programs capable of simulating intelligent human behavior. AI is currently everywhere around us, from self-driving cars and unmanned aerial vehicles to translation and investment software, as well as many other applications that are widespread in everyday life (Al-Salmi, 1999).

It can therefore be said that AI is an attempt to make computers or machines that operate through programming behave like humans in their thinking, actions, problem-solving, and practice of all aspects of daily life. This is achieved through studies conducted on humans, from which results are extracted that help explain human behaviour and are programmed for application to machines.

Characteristics of AI

AI entities have a set of characteristics and features that enable them to acquire a special autonomy, as follows:

I. The ability to absorb information: AI programs are characterized by their ability to absorb facts and information, store them, and encode them in databases using standard methods called knowledge representation. They then create a knowledge base and populate it with as much information and data as possible to address the problems and issues presented to them. Therefore, the ability of AI to understand and analyze inputs effectively, providing outputs that meet needs, means that robots can now learn continuously, automatically, and independently, without being subject to control and supervision (Youssef, 2022).

II. The ability to deal with incomplete information: One of the characteristics of AI is its unlimited ability to deal with incomplete information and find solutions through it. Perhaps this ability stems from the AI program's ability to learn from previous experiences and practices, as well as its flexibility in improving performance to correct and rectify errors. Logical thinking in AI is one of the different forms of thinking, as facts are deduced from the information available to it. Logical thinking corresponds to human probabilistic thinking, and both can address uncertain future circumstances that are likely to occur, such as self-driving cars that may encounter traditional road hazards and their ability to deal with these hazards in an optimal manner (Lutfi, 2021).

III. The ability to use the experimental method in problem solving: AI systems rely on the use of the experimental process by choosing a specific and suitable method for solving problems. It does not depend on a routine sequence of steps, and this important feature, which was created by the newly developed systems in AI, allows it to change the method if the first option does not quickly lead to the optimal solution (Ricardo, 2011).

Advantages of AI in the Criminal Field

AI plays a vital role in various areas of life, including criminal justice, as it can be used to combat multiple types of crime. This leads us to discuss the advantages and disadvantages of AI.

The fantastic progress in the field of AI technologies has enabled the development of programs with capabilities that exceed human capabilities in the criminal field. There is no doubt that it has brought justice and security to an unprecedented level. Therefore, we will discuss here some of the uses of AI in the criminal field, from the classification of criminals, the use of AI in crime prediction, and the identification of crime hotspots. In addition to its use in conducting searches to obtain criminal and scientific evidence, AI is also utilized in reconstructing crime scenes and assessing prisoners in correctional institutions.

I. Using AI in the classification of criminals: AI facilitates many tasks, especially in the legal field, where AI software contributes to the easy and objective classification of criminals, free from personal bias. There is no doubt that AI surpasses humans in this field, as machines are not susceptible to psychological influences, which reduces the margin of error in application.

II. Using AI to predict crime and identify crime hotspots: AI technologies help detect crimes and predict crime rates, types of crimes, and places that may become crime hotspots in the future. This is achieved through software algorithms that are fed specific data, which they analyze to produce results that help prevent anticipated crimes. For example, AI can be used to identify customers who purchase unusual quantities of chemicals that could be used in terrorist activities, such as the manufacture of hand grenades (Abul-Maati Sakr, 2021).

III. The use of AI in conducting searches to obtain criminal and scientific evidence. Searching homes involves looking for evidence of a crime in people's private spaces. It is one of the preliminary investigation procedures that the law gives to investigating judges, except for offenses caught in the act. These are given to judicial police officers under Article 41 of the Algerian Code of Criminal Procedure. This imposes restrictions that must be observed by the person conducting the search, in addition to the requirement that the search must relate to a crime that has been committed (Al-Aish, n.d.). For example, the Algerian Code of Criminal Procedure regulates the entry into and search of dwellings in Articles 44-48.

There are several models of security innovations for AI technologies in the field of inspection as a means of obtaining criminal and scientific evidence, including:

1. Ground-penetrating radar: This technology measures changes in the earth's layers to a depth of 205 meters below the surface by regularly measuring the reflection of electromagnetic waves to detect objects buried underground, such as drugs, weapons, and explosives. This technology is utilized by scientific police teams, forensic evidence teams, and forensic medicine teams that require conducting investigations and extracting evidence from beneath the earth's surface without resorting to digging and excavation. This system is characterized by its speed and accuracy (Abul-Maati Sakr, 2021).
2. Thermal cameras for night vision: These cameras are used effectively on roads and in areas in complete darkness, and can identify people, cars, and animals at a distance up to four times the range of headlights.
3. The use of AI in reconstructing crime scenes: Most crimes leave behind key elements: the perpetrator, the victim, the murder weapon, and the crime scene. The latter is considered a repository of the secrets of the crime, from which all the evidence emerges (Lazrak, 2017). Crime scene experts work to interpret how the crime occurred by examining signs and materials that hold significance and convey numerous facts, including multiple traces that vary from one crime to another.
4. Using AI to assess prisoners in correctional institutions: AI technologies can perform the tasks of evaluating prisoners in correctional institutions and studying their cases through reports that are entered into these systems. These systems analyze the reports and reach an impartial and transparent conclusion regarding conditional release or completion of the sentence. This could even extend to the creation and management of a prison using AI technologies without any human intervention.

The significant predictive power offered by AI tools will support decision-making related to crime scene reconstruction. A decision network model has been developed to predict the type of case based on inputs (evidence and scenario), thereby aiding in the solution of a case. A decision network model is defined as a probabilistic model that represents a set of variables and their dependencies through a graph. It is an ideal model for predicting probabilities. For example, a network can represent the probabilistic relationships between diseases and symptoms, as well as the probabilistic relationships between evidence and the type of crime. AI technologies can also help identify the perpetrator. Through complex programming and the use of specific algorithms, we can uncover the mystery of any incident by photographing the crime scene and studying the health condition of the suspect to prove their ability to commit the crime. Despite the critical role that AI technologies can play in the criminal justice field, the level of use of these technologies varies among countries due to differences in technological research and applications.

Disadvantages of AI in the Criminal Field

With the rapid advancement of AI, some essential challenges and downsides may arise from the use of this advanced technology. Elon Musk, the owner of X and founder of Open AI, has stated, "AI will be far more dangerous than nuclear weapons." Therefore, this chapter addresses the disadvantages and shortcomings of AI in the criminal field, including the violation of privacy, hacking, and tampering with the private accounts of individuals, companies, and banks, the use of AI by terrorists, and the possibility of deceiving AI systems.

I. Violation of privacy: The violation of privacy and human privacy is one of the most important negatives that will result from the growth of AI without regulation and the establishment of legal controls and limits. All current technological services, which are becoming increasingly widespread, require users to agree to allow AI software to extract specific data from either the user's phone or the device used to access that technology, analyze that data, and obtain the user's interests for use in many purposes, the most important of which are commercial. Governments' use of AI technologies in the process of collecting and controlling data is not always positive, as it can be implemented in a biased manner, making it a tool for entrenching inequality and infringing on freedoms (Abul-Maati, 2021).

II. Hacking and tampering with the private accounts of individuals, companies, and banks. There are malicious technologies based on AI software that can hack, crack codes, and threaten the private accounts of companies, individuals, and banks. A massive amount of malicious software, specializing in hacking and account intrusion, is available across thousands of platforms, spread across websites dedicated to hacking software. In fact, this software is now easily accessible for purchase through several websites specializing in encryption and decryption.

III. Terrorist use of AI: Terrorist groups have been able to exploit technological developments to carry out their terrorist operations in a focused manner by using social media to exchange content and communicate with selected groups of people who share the same ideas to achieve their terrorist strategy. This involves searching for information that terrorists seek to obtain, such as vital facilities, airports, and critical military sites, as well as how to conceal themselves, communicate, plan, and coordinate terrorist operations, thereby allowing them the freedom to plan precisely and coordinate comprehensively to launch specific terrorist attacks. Terrorist groups have also taken advantage of various applications of AI and used them for terrorist purposes. Their development and use of drones to carry explosives is clear evidence of this, not to mention their use in espionage, tracking, and monitoring targets in assassination operations that use facial recognition systems to identify the person to be eliminated and carry out assassinations in a way that is difficult to trace (Gherkan, 2024).

IV. The possibility of deceiving AI systems: Security agencies in developed countries tend to rely on AI systems to monitor and identify threats to national security and to predict developments that may occur around the world, such as revolutions or unrest. However, suppose hostile countries succeed in determining how these systems work. In that case, it becomes easier for them to deceive them by spreading false news, thereby misleading and leading them to false conclusions, and secretly creating an automatic double agent.

Rules of Criminal Liability Arising from AI Actions

The development of AI and the extent to which liability arising from its actions is recognized pose significant legal challenges and problems, as this entity enjoys a high degree of independence. When humans are entirely in charge of the decision-making process for AI, they can predict the consequences of these decisions and therefore bear responsibility for them. However, it is also conceivable that machines could be held responsible for certain harmful behaviors that constitute crimes, whose decisions are unpredictable and whose consequences cannot be avoided, based on deep and complex machine learning algorithms. Therefore, this section addresses the jurisprudential debate surrounding the attribution of criminal responsibility to AI, as well as the parties responsible for the criminal liability of AI entities and the penalties imposed on them, and finally, the extent to which there are grounds for permissibility and impediments to liability for AI entities.

Jurisprudential Trends Regarding the Attribution of Criminal Responsibility to AI

The concept of criminal liability for AI entities has raised several questions among jurists regarding the attribution of criminal liability to these entities. Jurisprudence is divided into two schools of thought: the first rejects the idea of criminal liability for AI technologies, while the second is in favor of holding AI technologies criminally liable.

I. The school of thought opposed the idea of criminal liability for the actions of AI: Most criminal legislation recognizes the ethical basis of criminal responsibility, and for a person to be held criminally liable, they must have had free will when committing the crime. Criminal responsibility is therefore limited to natural people. Charges can only be brought against normal people, as they are the only ones capable of bearing criminal responsibility. This is because the rules of criminal attribution relate primarily to legal personality, which can only be established for humans. This is normal because humans are characterized by awareness and perception of their actions. Proponents of this view, therefore, find it challenging to recognize AI technologies as criminally responsible, based on the following arguments:

1. The impossibility of attributing crime to AI entities due to their nature: Proponents of this view believe that the purpose of attribution is to hold the perpetrator accountable for their actions and subject them to the penalties prescribed by law. Since attribution is one of the pillars of criminal responsibility, it is based on the personal characteristics and subjective elements of the perpetrator, which means that the perpetrator must have the necessary capacity for the crime to be attributed to them. Jurisprudence has traditionally divided attribution into two interrelated parts. The first part relates to the material attribution made by the perpetrator regarding their act, as it is not sufficient for the crime to be established that criminal behavior occurred and the criminal result was achieved. Instead, it is also necessary that this result be attributed to that behavior, in the sense that there is a causal relationship between them. The second part is moral attribution, which requires a voluntary link between the perpetrator and his crime, as the latter is only attributed to the perpetrator if he can perceive and choose (Hallevy, 2016). Therefore, both types of attribution are essential conditions for criminal liability (Farid, 1981). AI entities are merely machines without free will and cannot make choices. Suppose the basis of criminal responsibility is free will and freedom of choice. In that case, if the perpetrator lacks free will and freedom of choice, criminal liability cannot be established against them. If a robot commits a criminal act, its lack of will negates criminal liability, which can only be established if the robot had, at the time of committing the crime, both consciousness and awareness on the one hand and the ability to choose on the other. Furthermore, robots are subject to commands and instructions through programming and therefore do not have free will or freedom of choice.
2. The philosophy of criminal punishment conflicts with the recognition of criminal responsibility for AI and the inapplicability of traditional penalties: criminal punishment aims to achieve deterrence in both its general and specific forms, according to the conventional school of thought, as well as to reform the offender, according to the positivist school of thought. Suppose we assume that AI entities have committed a crime, and we apply traditional penalties to them. In that case, this will not

achieve deterrence for other entities, nor will it accomplish the primary purpose of punishment, which is to inflict pain on the perpetrator of the crime. This will only be effective if the perpetrator is a human being. Therefore, it is inconceivable to impose traditional criminal penalties, such as the death penalty and imprisonment, on an AI entity, as it lacks the sensory aspects of pain or the fear of punishment (Idlibi, 2023), which contradicts the philosophy of punishment and criminalization.

3. AI crimes are an application of the theory of moral agency: traditional jurisprudence was applied because AI devices are indiscriminate and lack perception. This means that their use in committing a crime is nothing more than an application of the theory of moral agency, which states that a moral agent is someone who exploits others to carry out a crime, thereby making them a tool in their hands to achieve the elements on which the crime is based. The moral agent carries out the crime through others who are well-intentioned or not criminally responsible, such as the insane or minors (Ibrahim, 2020). He is the one who pushes others to commit the crime, and is a tool in his hands that he uses to commit the crime. The legislator did not differentiate between the means used by the perpetrator to commit the crime, and this applies to humans as a means of committing the crime, so criminal responsibility is negated and attributed to the moral agent.
4. Non-liability of designers, producers, and owners of robot users: The majority of jurists object to granting legal personality to AI, as these intelligent systems have not developed to the level of programming found in humans. Furthermore, the concept of granting legal personality is a human-centric approach to regulating transactions within the framework of human relations, which is inconceivable in the context of intelligent machines (Karim, 2022). This may be the reason why experts and specialists in the field of AI from 14 European countries sent a strongly worded memorandum to stop the debate in the European Parliament on denying robots legal personality, as this would entail them enjoying other rights, such as marriage and the right to own property. They consider this idea to be a ploy by owners or manufacturers to evade legal responsibility, in addition to the fact that the concept itself poses a threat to public order.

5. The criminality of AI entities violates the principle of criminal legality: Supporters of this view believe that attributing crime to an AI entity violates the principle of criminal legality and punishment. Referring to the penal code in positive law, we find that it addresses natural persons who have the capacity for cognition, as most legal texts begin with the word 'person...' or 'persons shall be punished...' and so on. The text does not mention AI entities (Idlibi, 2023).

II. The trend in favor of criminal liability for AI technologies: The failure of traditional jurisprudence to recognize the legal personality of AI stems from the view that robots fall within the legal definition of objects and are therefore not subject to criminal liability. However, contemporary legislation has taken a different view, granting robots limited legal personality. This is due to the tremendous development of AI applications, which have become capable of learning and making decisions by processing data within them, and robots have become capable of reacting independently of their creators (Derbal, 2022; Abul-Maati Sakr, 2021). As a result, there have been many calls to grant legal personality to AI, thereby enabling it to acquire rights and assume obligations. Proponents of this view have argued that for an AI entity to be held criminally liable, it must be recognized as having legal personality. They have based their argument on several arguments and proofs, which we will examine in some detail.

1. Analogous to the legal personality of legal entities: AI systems have become more complex and play a significant role in society. For this reason, calls have emerged for them to have some form of legal personality. These calls originated from a comparison with legal entities, such as companies, institutions, and associations. Let's consider a legal entity to be a subject of law, distinct from a human body. We are dealing with a vessel of rights and duties, whereby robots become akin to companies, with each robot being registered in a register equivalent to the commercial register for companies and acquiring legal personality from the time of registration. From that time onwards, compensation can be sought for damage caused by the robot, and they bear criminal responsibility for their actions.
2. The absence of a correlation between legal personality and human characteristics: Legal personality, as defined by the positivist school, is the exclusive capacity to acquire rights, bear

duties, and participate in legal relationships protected by law to achieve specific objectives. It is therefore not linked to human characteristics. Legal personality was first granted to families, not individuals, and women, children, and slaves were denied it. On the other hand, following economic, social, and political developments, legal personality has been granted to non-humans, such as companies that lack any human characteristics. It has therefore become possible to grant legal personality to AI entities, as legal personality is independent and unrelated to humanity.

3. The possibility of replacing human cognition with artificial cognition: The astonishing development of robots has created a new entity that enjoys full consciousness and cognition through the sensory reception and understanding of data inputs. Currently, most robots can sense images, sounds, and touch, and these technologies can analyze that data through processes similar to those used by the human mind. Proponents of this view believe that if an AI entity can perceive and sense, it is only natural that criminal responsibility can be attributed to it. Furthermore, the lack of connection between decision-making by an AI entity and humans leads to the possibility of holding the AI entity accountable for those decisions (Abul-Maati, 2021).
4. The basis of criminal responsibility is criminal danger, not risk. Proponents of this approach deny the role of will in the commission of a crime, considering humans to be driven by their actions rather than their choices, and rejecting the principle of free will. According to them, criminals do not choose to commit crimes and are therefore not held accountable for their actions, but rather for their failure to fulfill their social responsibilities. Through his actions, the offender has revealed his criminal dangerousness. Therefore, according to the supporters of this approach, if an act committed by an AI entity results in a crime, it should be punished based on social responsibility, because their basis for responsibility is criminal dangerousness, regardless of fault.

Parties Responsible for the Criminal Liability of AI Entities and the Penalties Imposed on Them

Criminal liability is the legal consequence of a perpetrator committing a crime and being held accountable for the consequences of their criminal behavior, whether intentional or unintentional. Committing a crime does not necessarily lead to the punishment prescribed by law, unless the judge proves the perpetrator's criminal liability, as these modern entities have four parties associated with criminal liability in this type of crime. We will therefore address the parties involved in criminal responsibility for AI crimes, followed by the penalties prescribed for them (Bouali, 2016).

I. Parties involved in criminal responsibility for AI crimes: In this subsection, we will discuss the criminal liability of the manufacturer, the criminal liability of the owner or user, the criminal liability of the AI itself, and finally the criminal liability of third parties for AI crimes.

   1. Criminal liability of the manufacturer: It is well known that the Penal Code establishes a general principle whereby a natural person is held accountable for any criminal act they commit, unless there are grounds for criminal immunity. Legal entities are also criminally liable for crimes committed by their representatives, managers, or agents on their behalf or in their name. They are subject to fines, confiscation, and other measures prescribed for the crime. This does not prevent the court from simultaneously punishing the perpetrator of the crime personally with the penalty prescribed by law for the crime (Abdel Aleem, 2024). The criminal liability of an AI manufacturer is one of the most critical issues that arise when the latter commits any act that constitutes a crime under the law. Therefore, research into the criminal liability of the manufacturer was necessary to clarify the extent of its role in criminal liability, as it may protect itself through clauses mentioned in the user agreement. This is signed by the owner, who bears sole criminal responsibility for crimes committed through this entity (Attia, 2023). The entity operates with AI, and the manufacturer relinquishes responsibility for any crimes committed before it. However, a crime may occur because of a programming error by the AI programmer. A programmer may release AI technology with defects that lead to crimes and is

therefore criminally liable for any resulting harm. A distinction must be made between whether his behavior was intentional or not, to determine whether the crime was committed intentionally or by mistake, as the penalties for each are different. The manufacturer is also responsible for complying with specific standards when developing AI programs, the most important of which is that they must include safety and security guarantees, i.e., the product must be free of defects that could endanger those who use it, in addition to being compatible with the values and traditions of society. The manufacturer, therefore, bears criminal responsibility for crimes committed by the AI it has manufactured in the event of any crime resulting from manufacturing defects.

2. Criminal liability of the owner or user: The owner or user is defined as the person who owns and operates AI technologies. Therefore, such technologies may be misused for purposes other than their intended use, resulting in acts that constitute crimes under the law (Al-Desouki, 2021). In this case, we must distinguish between three possibilities:
   a. The crime was committed solely by the owner or user. Had it not been for their actions, the crime would not have been committed, and they would bear full criminal responsibility. An example of this is when the user or owner disables the automatic control of a self-driving car and relies solely on the voice instructions issued by the AI program, thereby becoming the sole controller of the vehicle. If the program issues a warning with a specific command to avoid an accident and the individual fails to carry out this command, then criminal liability falls solely on them (Dahshan, 2020).
   b. The crime occurs because of the owner's behavior in conjunction with another party, such as the manufacturer, the AI technology itself, or another external party. For example, when a car owner modifies the operating commands in a self-driving car with the assistance of a specialist in this field to commit a crime and deny criminal responsibility, blaming the car and its manufacturer instead. In this case, criminal responsibility is shared. We note that the Algerian Penal Code addresses criminal participation and contribution in Articles 41 to 46, defining cases of involvement in a crime

as assistance, aiding, or providing accommodation or shelter for a meeting of criminals (Articles 41-46 of Ordinance No. 156-66, 1966). While the Egyptian Penal Code defines cases of participation in a crime in Article 40 of Law 58 of 1937 (Law No. 58 of 1937, as amended and supplemented by Law No. 95 of 2003).

3. Criminal liability for AI itself :Talking about AI committing a crime on its own is currently considered a kind of fantasy, and without a programming error as a result of self-development in the AI system that operates in it and is capable of thinking and issuing decisions, but this is possible because it is linked to the data produced by evolution and science fiction, and therefore It is possible to develop perceptions of the occurrence of the crime by the AI itself as follows:
    a. AI may commit the crime itself without the fault of the programmers, manufacturers, its owner, or any other third party. In this case, the intelligent robot or AI is exclusively criminally responsible.
    b. The participation of another party to the AI in committing the criminal act and thus being an accomplice in this crime. An example of this is when smart mobile phone users root their phone, which allows specific applications to control the device, potentially leading to it being destroyed programmatically.
4. Criminal liability of the external party for AI crimes :In addition to the owner and user, an external party may intervene in AI crimes, such that the latter enters the AI system through hacking or in any other way, controlling it, and exploiting it to commit the crime. In this case, we are faced with two possibilities (Al-Desouki, 2021):
    a. Joint criminal liability of the external party: The external party exploited a vulnerability in AI to commit a crime, and this vulnerability was the result of the owner or manufacturer's negligence in this technology. Criminal liability here is shared between the external party and a person who was negligent in exploiting this loophole. An example of this is giving the owner of the AI access to the system controlling AI technology for this external party, which made it easier for them to issue orders to AI.

b. Full criminal liability of the external party: This is when the external party exploits a vulnerability in AI without the assistance or negligence mentioned in the previous case. So full criminal liability falls on this external party, an example of which is the external party's penetration of the electronic cloud "*The electron cloud is the region of negative charge surrounding the nucleus of the atom, associated with the atomic orbit, and the electron cloud describes the region containing electrons, and the use of the phrase 'electron cloud' first appeared around 1925 AD, when Erwin Schrödinger and Werner Heisenberg were looking for a way to describe the exact position of electrons in the atom, so that the electrons orbit the nucleus in the same way as the planets orbit the sun. The electrons orbit the nucleus in the same way that the planets orbit the sun. In the electron cloud model, there are regions where electrons are most likely to be located. Still, it is theoretically possible for the electron to be located anywhere, including inside the nucleus*"(Haskar Murad, 2022). Through which matters are stored and sent to AI technology. It issues orders to the AI to commit a specific crime, such as giving software orders to attack people with certain characteristics (skin color - a specific uniform).

II. Penalties applied to crimes of AI entities: The principle of criminal legality is the basis on which criminal law is based, as Article 1 of the Algerian Penal Code stipulates that: "There is no crime, punishment, or security measures without a law." (Article 1 of Ordinance No. 156-66, 1966). Accordingly, it is not permissible to criminalize an act and impose punishment on its perpetrator unless a prior legal text explicitly permits it. Upon committing that act, and this is what various comparative legislations have settled on from this standpoint, we discuss the penalties that can be applied regarding AI crimes. Then, we examine the fines imposed on the owner and user of AI, and finally, the penalties imposed on the AI entities themselves.

1. Sanctions imposed on the AI entity factory: The factory means the producer who is more knowledgeable and capable of controlling and dealing with AI technologies by programming them correctly. He can be controlled on the one hand and mitigate his risks by following safety controls and procedures that prevent

these technologies from deviating from them, thus reducing the possibility of committing crimes in the future.

The penalties imposed on an AI technology factory vary depending on the number of crimes committed by AI entities, regardless of the order of criminal liability, whether they result from negligence on the part of the factory in setting controls over it, or whether the criminal liability stems from intent. That is, the factory deliberately developed a program that makes the AI entity commit the criminal act, and thus traditional penalties can be imposed on the factory (Youssef, 2022). The severity of the fines imposed on AI entities varies according to the gravity of the crime committed by these entities, which the factory neglected to prevent when setting controls to prevent such acts. These penalties range from death, imprisonment, or a fine, depending on the seriousness and gravity of the criminal act and the severe damage it causes (Mohamed Saeed, 2022).

2. Penalties imposed on the owner of the AI entity: The possessor or user of an AI entity is necessarily its owner, and therefore, the use of AI techniques to commit a crime by the owner requires the application of criminal penalties. These penalties vary according to the type of crime committed, as the user who possesses the AI entity is the person who can exploit it. In committing criminal acts against individuals and property, these crimes are described as intentional offenses. Incorrect operation of AI technology may also result in criminal behavior. In such cases, the user's responsibility is considered assumed when the manufacturer provides the method of operation and security guarantees. AI entities may also commit crimes due to the owner's negligence, and such actions can be described as unintentional crimes or unintentional liability. On the other hand, the owner or user of the AI entity, once ownership of the intelligent machine is transferred to him, is criminally responsible for all crimes that it may commit. This requires imposing the appropriate punishment on him for that, considering the distinction between crimes committed by AI entities themselves, of their own free will and independent of the person who owns it or the user, and those caused by the owner or user due to negligence. This requires the application of appropriate penalties to the owner or user. What are the penalties that can be imposed on the manufacturer or

producer of these innovative technologies? They are classified according to the degree of seriousness by AI entities, ranging from death to life imprisonment, aggravated imprisonment, imprisonment, or a fine, depending on the degree of severity and gravity. The resulting damage, in addition to supplementary penalties, aggravating circumstances, and recidivism (Al-Desouki, 2021).

3. Sanctions are imposed on the AI entity itself: It is not possible to talk about penalties applied to the AI entity itself without recognizing its legal personality. The focus of criminal responsibility, as previously mentioned, is awareness and discrimination, and the penalty cannot be imposed unless this technology can be shown to act independently of the parties connected to it (the manufacturer and the user).

In this regard, we note that the significant advancements in the manufacturing and programming of AI systems have endowed them with the capacity to develop autonomously, thereby creating the possibility of committing crimes independently, without external interference. Therefore, it was necessary to find penalties that are compatible with the nature of this technology. It is not envisaged to apply traditional criminal penalties; rather, it is intended to introduce modifications. On the robot, for example, the perpetrator of the crime could disable it or change its use.

III. Looking forward to the future, contemporary jurisprudence sees the necessity of searching for alternative punishments to confront the potential imminent danger. Examples of these punishments include (Idlibi, 2023):

a. Dissolution or suspension and confiscation, which are punishments similar to execution for a natural person.
b. Financial penalties are paid to the State Treasury and deducted from the financial liability of AI.
c. Penalties involving deprivation of rights and involving measures of qualification and reprogramming or withdrawal of the driving license in the case of self-driving cars.

The Availability of Reasons for Permissibility and Impediments to Liability for AI Entities

Criminal acts are often accompanied by objective circumstances that render them permissible, thereby removing their criminal character. Although they contain the elements of the crime, this behavior is acceptable and is not punishable (Baghcham, 2023). These circumstances are known as the reasons for permissibility and are similar to the impediments to liability in not punishing her.

I. The availability of reasons for permissibility for AI entities: The Algerian legislator, like other comparative legislation, limits the reasons for permissibility to the act ordered or authorized by law and the legitimate defense. We address the right of legitimate defense of the AI entity, and the right of the owner or user to defend the AI entity.

1. The right of legitimate defense for the AI entity: the right to legitimate defense in Algerian law and the right to legitimate defense in Egyptian law were discussed.
    a. The right of legitimate defense of the AI entity in Algerian law: Algerian law regulates the right to legitimate defense through Articles 39/2 and 40 of the Algerian Penal Code (Article 39(2) and Article 40 of Ordinance No. 156-66, 1966). This indicates that the Algerian legislator limited the right to legitimate defense to a natural person to protect themselves, their property, or the life or property of others, so there is no indication that this right is granted to entities. Others, even implicitly.
    b. The right of legitimate defense for AI entities in Egyptian law: According to the Egyptian Penal Code (Law No. 58 of 1937, as amended and supplemented by Law No. 95 of 2003), AI entities enjoy this right. The law grants this to the natural person only, and not to other entities, as stated in Article 245 of the Egyptian Penal Code, which prohibits punishing someone who kills or injures others in defense of themselves or their property, or for the benefit of someone else or their property. Article 246 of this law stipulates that the right to legitimate defense is an exception to the original rule. Therefore, Egyptian law does not recognize the legitimate defense of the AI entity at all, because if it

recognizes this right for a robot and kills a human being who assaulted it, we will equate the life of a human with the life of a machine.

2. The right of legitimate defense of the AI entity for the owner or user: Comparative legislation has unanimously agreed to address the natural person exclusively regarding the right to legitimate defense of oneself, money, others, or one's money. However, in practice, if an intelligent robot can distinguish between the act of assaulting the owner and the act of defense it performs, it can defend the owner (the natural person). If the robot exceeds the defense, its owner will be held accountable for this violation.

II. The availability of liability barriers for AI entities: If the reasons for permissibility relate to the legal and moral element of the criminal act, then the impediments to liability relate to the ethical element, and therefore, they do not affect the crime, but rather only prevent the application of the criminalization text to the person who committed the criminal act. Accordingly, the presence of a reason for permissibility on the part of the person committing the criminal act increases the criminal liability of this person. We also find this result in some cases, such as impediments to liability of a personal nature, as this is due to the absence of a moral element of the crime.

Jurisprudence goes on to propose rules regarding impediments to criminal liability for an AI entity, so that a robot can benefit from exemption from punishment if an external party interferes in its behavior, leading it to deviate from its usual and programmed behavior. Referring to the Algerian legislator, we find that it addressed the impediments to liability in Articles 47, 48, and 49 of the Algerian Penal Code, which are insanity, youth, and coercion. On this basis, and to apply these rules related to the impediments to liability for a natural person with respect to AI entities, the intelligent robot must have the ability to perceive, distinguish, and choose behaviors and actions. We believe that AI entities cannot be granted the right of legitimate defense except if the aggressor against this entity is a being who is not a human person, and in the sense of violating the intelligent robot, the right of legitimate defense if the aggressor is of its own gender, and this right cannot be granted to the intelligent robot to protect its owner or user. Suppose the aggressor against its owner is a natural person. As for AI benefiting from not being punished if it commits crimes, rules must be established through which the intelligent entities that benefit from this feature are determined, in addition to the entities for which punishment cannot be lifted.

Conclusion

The current era is marked by the widespread adoption of AI technologies across various fields of life. Therefore, researching crimes related to these technologies has become an inevitable necessity to hold criminals responsible for crimes committed through AI, in addition to the need to codify the conditions of AI so that it can be held criminally accountable for the crimes committed through it. At the conclusion of this chapter on the issue of criminal liability arising from AI crimes, we reached a set of results and recommendations, which we present as follows for the results: Despite the widespread use of AI technologies in all areas of life, criminal legislation did not include a definition of this technology, and most definitions focused on AI being machine science or engineering that mimic human intelligence. These entities are characterized by characteristics that enable them to acquire a special personality, the most prominent of which are: the ability to absorb information, deal with missing information, use the experimental method in solving problems, and their ability to make inferences. Recognition by some comparative legislation of the legal personality of AI entities so that they may be held criminally liable for the criminal acts and conduct resulting therefrom as self-contained entities. The issue of establishing criminal liability for crimes committed by these semi-complex technologies arises due to their multiplicity of parties, ranging from the factory to the owner or user, and extending to the AI entities themselves and external parties.

Holding these entities criminally accountable results in punishment. This punishment must be compatible with the nature of these innovative technologies. The right of legitimate defense can be granted to these entities only if their aggressor is a physical entity, that is, an unnatural being. Inadequacy of the provisions of the General Criminal Code in accommodating, regulating, and determining criminal liability and punishment for offenses resulting from the use of AI entities.

Based on the results obtained, the following recommendations can be made: current criminal legislation must keep pace with the development in the field of AI by introducing legislative amendments that are compatible with the new crimes that the use of innovative applications may cause. Seek appropriate penalties for crimes resulting from the use of AI, and increase the penalty if it comes to the manufacturers and owners of these entities for not escaping punishment and establishing controls and standards that determine the manufacture, programming, and use of AI machines and programs to avoid committing serious mistakes by these entities and paying attention to the seriousness of the issue considering the wide spread of these entities by holding scientific seminars and conferences to contribute to avoiding the danger coming from technology.

References

Abdel Aleem, M. B. (2024). *Criminal liability arising from artificial intelligence offenses. Journal of Legal and Economic Studies*, *10*(1), 1292.

Abu al-Fadl, I. M. (1968). *Lisan al-Arab.* (Vol. 8). Dar al-Sadr.

Abul-Maati Sakr, W. (2021). Criminal liability arising from artificial intelligence crimes: A futuristic analytical study. *Journal of the Spirit of Law*, *(96)*, 41.

Al-Aish, F. (n.d.). *Commentary on the Algerian Code of Criminal Procedure between theory and practice.* Al-Badr Press.

Al-Desouki, M. M. A. (2022). Crimes of artificial intelligence and independent electronic legal personality: A comparative study. *Journal of Legal and Economic Research*, *(81)*, 1180.

Al-Najjar, F. (2010). *Management information systems: A managerial perspective* (4th ed.). Dar Al-Hamid for Publishing and Distribution.

Al-Salmi, A. R. (1999). *Information systems and artificial intelligence.* Dar Al-Manajah for Publishing and Distribution.

Article 1 of Ordinance No. 156-66 of 18 Safar 1386, corresponding to 8 June 1966, containing the Algerian Penal Code, as amended and supplemented, Official Gazette of the Republic of Algeria No. 49, 1966.

Article 39(2) and Article 40 of Ordinance No. 156-66 of 18 Safar 1386, corresponding to 8 June 1966, containing the Algerian Penal Code, as amended and supplemented, Official Gazette of the Republic of Algeria No. 49, 1966.

Articles 41-46 of of Ordinance No. 156-66 of 18 Safar 1386, corresponding to 8 June 1966, the Algerian Penal Code, as amended. *Official Gazette of the Republic of Algeria*, No. 49 (1966).

Attia Dabisha, M. N. H. (2023). Criminal liability arising from artificial intelligence offences. *Journal of the Spirit of Laws*, *35*(102), 2303.

Baghcham, Z. (2023). *Lectures on the general criminal law scale – General theory of crime* (Pedagogical publication). Faculty of Law, University of Glizan.

Bouali, S., & Rachid, D. (2016). *Commentary on the Algerian Penal Code - General Section.* Dar Belkis Publishing.

Dahshan, Y. I. (2020). Criminal responsibility for artificial intelligence crimes. *Journal of Sharia and Law*, *82*, 109.

Derbal, S. (2022). Problems of recognising the legal personality of an intelligent robot. *Journal of Jurisprudence*, *14*(29), 459.

Farid, H. (1981). The Philosophical Underpinnings of Criminal Responsibility: A Comparative Study, Arab Renaissance House, Cairo, p. 561.

Gherkan, A. M. (2024). International cooperation to address the threat of terrorism using artificial intelligence. In *Proceedings of the First International Forum: The Future of Artificial Intelligence: Legal and Ethical Challenges* (p. 24). Arab Democratic Centre.

Hallevy, G. (2016). The criminal liability of the artificial intelligence entities—From science fiction to legal social control. *Akron Law Journal*, 177.

Haskar Murad, B. O. (2022). Problems of applying criminal liability provisions to artificial intelligence offences. *Journal of Law and Humanities*, (1): 200.

Ibn Zakariya, A. A.-H. (1979). *Muajam al-Muqasim al-Lughayas* (Vol. 8). Dar al-Fikr for Printing, Publishing and Distribution.

Ibrahim, A. I. M. (2020). *Criminal liability arising from artificial intelligence errors in the UAE legislation – A comparative study* (PhD thesis, Ain Shams University).

Idlibi, O. M. M. (2023). *Criminal responsibility for artificial intelligence acts* (Master's thesis, College of Law, Qatar University).

Karim, S. A. (2022). *Legal regulation of artificial intelligence – A comparative study* (Doctoral dissertation, Karbala University of Iraq), 117–118.

Law No. 58 of 1937, as amended and supplemented by Law No. 95 of 2003.

Law No. 58 of 1937, as amended and supplemented by Law No. 95 of 2003 containing the Egyptian Penal Code.

Lazrak, J. M. (2017). Technical and technical research procedures of the scientific police at the crime scene. *Matoun Magazine*, *10*(1), 673.

Lutfi, K. (2021). *Artificial intelligence and its civil and criminal protection* (1st ed.). Dar Al-Fikr Al-Jami'i.

McCarthy, J. (n.d.). In *Wikipedia.* Retrieved from https://en.wikipedia.org/wiki/John_McCarthy_ (computer_scientist). Acceded on July 29, 2025.

Mohamed Saeed, W. S. El-Din. (2022). Criminal liability arising from artificial intelligence applications. *Journal of Legal and Economic Sciences*, *02*(64), 526.

Ordinance No. 156-66 of 18 Safar 1386 corresponding to 8 June 1966, containing the Algerian Penal Code, as amended and supplemented. *Official Gazette of the Republic of Algeria*, No. 49.

Ordinance No. 156-66, Article 39(2) and Article 40, Algerian Penal Code, as amended. *Official Gazette of the Republic of Algeria*, No. 49 (1966).

Ordinance No. 156-66, Article 42, Algerian Penal Code, as amended. *Official Gazette of the Republic of Algeria*, No. 49 (1966).

Ricardo, C. (2011). *Logique pour l'informatique et pour l'intelligence artificielle*. Hermes Science Publications.

Yassin, G. (2012). *Fundamentals of management information systems and information technology* (Vol. 1). Dar Al-Manawah for Publishing and Distribution.

Youssef, M. M. (2022). *Artificial intelligence crimes: The new criminals*. New University House, Alexandria.

Chapter 4

Ear-Prints as a Means of Innovative Biological Evidence in Criminal Investigation

Walid Mahmoud Khalilia *
Forensic Science Department, Al-Istiqlal University, Jericho, Palestine

Abstract

To achieve justice, modern forensic physical evidence has increasingly been used to solve most crimes more quickly and effectively. Criminals are constantly developing new methods to circumvent traditional methods of criminal investigation, particularly physical evidence. This chapter focuses on ear-prints as modern forensic evidence, discussing the human external ear characteristics, the reasons for its adoption as forensic biological evidence, its importance in crime detection, and some of the challenges facing this field of forensic evidence. This chapter also presents some historical criminal cases in which ear-prints were used to solve crimes. It further explores the processes of handling ear-prints at crime scenes, which include searching for and documenting them, as well as the subsequent appropriate methods for collecting, preserving, and recognizing ear-prints. The characteristics of the auricle, such as size, shape, and curvature, as well as whether the earlobe is attached, make this organ an important piece of forensic evidence for solving criminal cases in the judicial system. The use of ear-prints in criminal identification is relatively new compared to other traditional techniques such as fingerprinting. This chapter explains the potential locations of ear-prints at a crime scene, whether visible or hidden, particularly in burglary cases, where ear-prints are relatively common. It also describes the mechanisms of searching for hidden ear-prints at a crime scene, and

* Corresponding Author's Email: khaliliawalid@gmail.com

In: Frontiers of Forensic Science: Innovation, Technology, and Justice
Editor: Walid M. Khalilia
ISBN: 979-8-90134-160-5

how to detect them. The study then demonstrates the importance of photographing and documenting the ear-prints before beginning the process of collecting them by forensic experts and technicians. This chapter also explains how traditional methods, similar to those used for fingerprints, are applied to collect ear-prints, although other practical new methods such as the 3D ERS system, may offer superior results. Therefore, ear-prints should be considered forensic for investigations. On the other hand, this field is limited, as the number of cases in which ear-prints have been used in criminal investigations is small. Although this technique has historically been effective in identifying suspects in several criminal cases, it has not gained as wide acceptance in the criminal justice system as other forms of evidence, due to the difficulties in locating the ear-prints location and lifting the entire ear-print from the crime scene. Therefore, the study concluded that it is necessary to continue researching new and advanced methods and developing traditional ones in this field. Ear-prints can be used as modern, complementary forensic biological evidence in criminal investigations. To enhance credibility of this kind of evidence, forensic experts and technicians must be educated and trained in the field of ear-prints, and scientific research must be supported for development. In addition, standardizing procedures for handling ear-prints is important for their acceptance in criminal courts.

Keywords: ear-print, forensic identification, crime scene investigation, biological forensic evidence

Introduction

Scientific and technological progress is a characteristic of the world we live in today and is evident across multiple fields. Humanity has been able to use this scientific and technological progress to serve society by facilitating and developing services and bridging distances. As a result, people have become increasingly eager to learn about modern scientific and technological techniques and use them in various areas of society. Criminals have also been able to use the benefits of scientific and technological progress to serve their criminal plans. Thus, their criminal activities have become more widespread, harmful, dangerous, heinous, and deadly to society, whether from a physical, economic, social, or security perspective, than before, during earlier times when these modern scientific and technological techniques were unavailable. There is no doubt that punishing an accused person for committing a crime and thus protecting various societal interests requires proving that the individual committed the crime. Otherwise, it is impossible to punish them.

Criminal justice is not affected by a criminal escaping punishment as much as it is by the conviction of an innocent person or the unjustified infringement of individual rights and freedoms guaranteed by the constitution and laws. One of the greatest challenges posed by modern technologies used by perpetrators in committing crimes lies in the difficulty of detecting such offenses. These crimes are often carried out using sophisticated methods, making it difficult to identify and track down offenders through traditional investigative approaches, particularly given the limited capabilities available to solve these crimes. For this reason, security agencies in various countries have sought, and continue to seek, to use modern scientific techniques to verify a person's identity and identify the perpetrators of various crimes, given the advanced capabilities of these technologies in identity verification (ALzwae, 2019).

Through the centuries, means of proof has gone through many stages of development, especially in forensic cases. They have evolved from relying on primitive methods such as confessions and eyewitness testimony to using the most accurate and sophisticated methods to detect the identity of criminals. The range of evidence is no longer limited, and the judicial system has evolved with the introduction of modern scientific methods to uncover and identify the perpetrators of crimes. We are now witnessing an advanced reality regarding the use of modern methods of proof, especially in the field of forensic prints and impressions, such as fingerprints, ear-prints, eye-prints, voiceprints, teeth-prints, lip-prints, facial-prints, footprints, brain-prints, and even DNA prints. The emergence of these modern methods has had a significant impact on various judicial systems by reshaping or limiting the authority of criminal judges (Andrea, 2016; Krishnan et al., 2016).

Ear-prints are one of the technologies that may help criminal justice agencies identify perpetrators, thereby enforcing the law and achieving security and tranquility in society. This is due to the physical characteristics or traits of an ear-print, which vary from one person to another. However, the use of ear-prints to detect crimes and their perpetratorsraises challenges related to the extent to which it respects various human rights guaranteed by the laws and constitutions of various countries. This is particularly true regarding the rights to privacy, confidentiality, human dignity, and the inviolability of the body, including the right to protection from objectionable collection of physical evidence. Furthermore, revealing an ear-print and the information it contains may reveal a person's secrets, such as their medical condition and ethnic origin. Such matters undoubtedly fall within the scope of the sanctity of an individual's private life. In addition, questions remain regarding how effectiveear-prints are in verifying and identifying the perpetrator of a crime? Convicting and punishing a person for a crime requires that the verdict be based on conclusive, definitive evidence that leaves no room for suspicion or possibility. The use of this technology should only be permitted within the framework of legal texts that permit its use in a manner that ensures the protection of human rights and freedoms, prevents infringement, and serves the investigative interest in solving the crime (ALzwae, 2019).

Ear-prints began to be used after scientific experiments proved their effectiveness in criminal investigation. Alphonse Bertillon conducted these experiments in 1879, during which he demonstrated that ear-prints differ from one person to another, and even within the same person, they differ between the right and the left ear. He himself stated the difficulty of finding such prints given that the ear does not typically touch crime scene surfaces. He said that ear prints are often in places where the perpetrator might seek to eavesdrop and ensure that there are no people at the crime scene, or they might be in narrow places. In 1949, Alfred Victor developed a system for classifying the ear, similar to the fingerprint system. He used innovative imaging methods and a complete formation of the ear on paper. He created methods to help him in this imaging process, and he saved these images arranged in special records. He published a book on determining a person's personality through the ear. Fritz Hirschi first discovered ear-prints and their use for identification in 1965 (Al-Maaytah, 2007).

The area of forensic science known as "forensic evidence of ear-print" focuses on gathering and comparing earmarks — which are typically left at crime scenes— with ear-prints taken from the ears of persons of interest under carefully monitored circumstances. According to anthropometric research and empirical data, the shapes that an outer ear leaves behind are highly distinctive and enable the presentation of evidence with a significant degree of reliability regarding the identity of individual who left them (Champod, 2009).

Meijerman et al. (2004) reviewed the literature on ear-print categorization and individualization based on findings from an initial ear-print investigation. The use of ear-prints in forensic investigations was discussed, along with their potential and limitations. The authors also examined the distinctions between excluding a suspect, locating a suspect at a crime scene, and connecting crimes using prints found at various locations.

An ear-print can be defined as a form of biological evidence that represents a two-dimensional shape on a surface created by the impression of waxes and oils from the skin of the human external ear under applied pressure (Kaushal, & Kaushal, 2011). Ear-prints can be used as evidence to connect a perpetrator to the scene because of the unique and individual features of human outer ear. In both the United States and Europe, comparable ear-print evidence has been used to link numerous offenses, leading to the conviction of many accused burglars (Krishan and Kanchan, 2025).

However, due to the subjective process of individualizing earmarks and the absence of standardized norms and ethical guidelines, ear-print evidence in legal proceedings around the world has been criticized (Krishan and Kanchan, 2025). Numerous studies around the world have concluded that ear measurements can be used to identify individuals in different societies. The study by Agrawal (2023) revealed that most parameters showed a high degree of variation among individuals. Another study conducted by Biwasaka et al. (2024) aimed to classify outer ear morphology for human identification in forensic investigations. A three-dimensional (3D) homologous model of the ear was created, and morphological variations were visualized using principal component analysis (PCA). Areas showing significant individual differences across the entire ear were identified. The findings show that the reference images used in this chapter for the morphological classification of ears are applicable (Biwasaka et al. 2024).

New possibilities for personal identification and verification have been made possible by developments in the field of biometrics. External ear features have been identified as a reliable biometric measure for identification and verification in a new model proposed by Gupta et al. (2023). Several features are extracted from ear samples for this model, which is then fed into a support vector machine (SVM) and a single-shot classifier. The given candidate sample is recognized by these classifiers, which are then subsequently validated against a known sample. This model is unique because it uses a lightweight, straightforward model that is simple to apply on biometric terminals without requiring large datasets or multiple samples. The study shows that the suggested approach works well and has a lot of promise. Using a single-shot classifier and SVM, they were able to identify and confirm ear-prints with a high degree of accuracy. An accuracy of 97.857% was achieved by combining the single-shot model with an orientated gradient histogram feature extractor. The proposed approach proved effective in a variety of identification and verification applications, including forensic science, access control systems, and personalized healthcare (Gupta et al. 2023).

The significance of this chapter arises from the continued growth in criminal offences, as crime rates have increased and evolved significantly, particularly organized felonies in which perpetrators resort to hiding their traces. Offenders are increasingly adopting new strategies to eliminate traditional clues, such as wearing gloves to hide fingerprint marks. Therefore, it is necessary to continue searching for new methods and evidence that will help criminal investigators identify the perpetrators. Accordingly, this chapter focuses on the role and status of ear-prints as biological evidence in criminal investigations.

This chapter discusses various issues related to ear-prints, such as their characteristics, importance, detection, location at a crime scene, collection, preservation, recognition, analysis, admissibility in court, and the challenges facing their use.

The Morphology and Characteristics of the External Ear

In order to understand the diverse features that produce the ear-print, one must first become acquainted with the auricle's morphology. The external ear consists of the external auditory canal and the auricle (pinna), which has a complex anatomical structure. The pinna folds in on itself, resulting in protuberances and depressions that give the external ear its distinctive and unique shape. Its form varies greatly in size and attachment (Deepak and Kumar, 2016; Attalla, et al., 2020). Consisting mostly of a fibro-cartilaginous structure covered by skin, the pinna averages approximately 60 to 65 mm along its major axis and 30 to 35 mm along its minor axis, although its size can vary significantly among individuals. The only part that does not have a cartilaginous structure is the earlobe, located at the lower portion of the auricle, which can occur in a variety of shapes (Verma, et al., 2016; Mustafa, et al., 2020).

The auricle is bent in many directions and is divided into a lateral and a medial surface. The lateral surface exhibits characteristic ridges and depressions, including the central auricle, which extends directly into the external auditory canal and is the most prominent. The outer helix, as well as the shape of the earlobe govern the overall contour of the auricle. An antihelix runs almost parallel to the outer helix but splits into two branches at the higher extremity. The inner helix and the lower of these two branches form the upper and left borders of the concha. In the anterior part of the auricle liesthe triangular tragus and between the tragus and the antitragus is the intertragic notch. The antitragus can be so pronounced that it is sometimes barely distinguishable. The antihelix occurs in a variety of shapes and can be classified into distinct types when combined with the lower and upper crust (Figure 1) (Kushal & Kushal, 2011; Mustafa, et al., 2020; Attalla, et al., 2020).

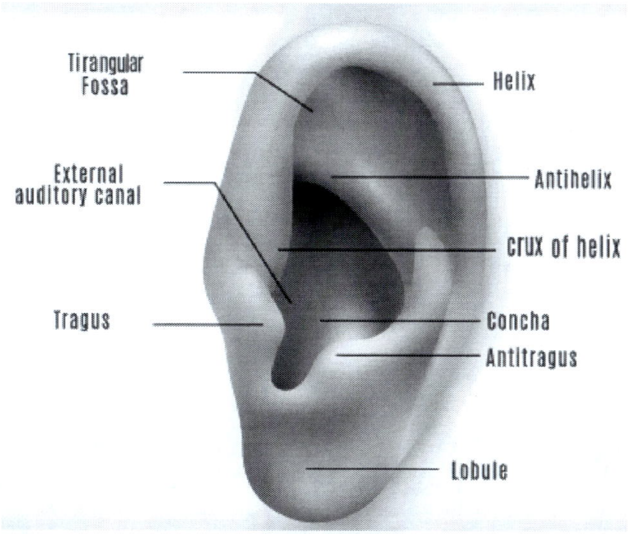

Figure 1. Morphological features of human external ear.

The shape and size of the auricle are influenced by genetic factors, particularly genes located on5q and 22q of chromosome11, which controlling the development of the first and second branchial arches responsible for auricle growth (Sforza, et al, 2009). Therefore, there are similarities and symmetry in term of measurements and morphological structures between the left and right auricles of the same individual (Wang, et al., 2010). The degree of auricular similarity among family members is positively correlated with their genetic proximity (Zhang, et al., 2020). However, environmental factors such as smoking and alcohol consumption during pregnancy can also contribute to asymmetry of external ears (Sforza. et al., 2009).

One of the organs that is unique to each individual in terms of position, size, and form is the auricle. The auricle's shape typically does not vary over the course of a person's life, and numerous studies conducted worldwide have shown that this organ is not particularly vulnerable to injury (Swift and Rutty, 2003; Zhang et al., 2020). Therefore, whin discussing the biological properties of the ear, we can refer to concepts such as stability, individuality, and indestructibility, , much like those used when describing the fingerprints.

Previous studies (Marinkovic, and Valjarevic, 2014; Yadav, 2017), classified auricles into four main shapes according to the form of their earlobe and outer edge (Figure 2):

1. Triangular shape: This type of external ear impression is shaped like a triangle, narrowing at the bottom near the earlobe and widening upwards.
2. Rectangular shape: This impression is shaped like a rhombus, with the width at the level of the upper helix and the earlobe being roughly equal.
3. Round shape: At tragus level, width of print exceeds half of its length, and both side edges of pinna are rounded and approximately equal.
4. Oval shape: The sides of the ear-prints are round, and the width of the print at tragus level is less than half the length of the ear pinna.

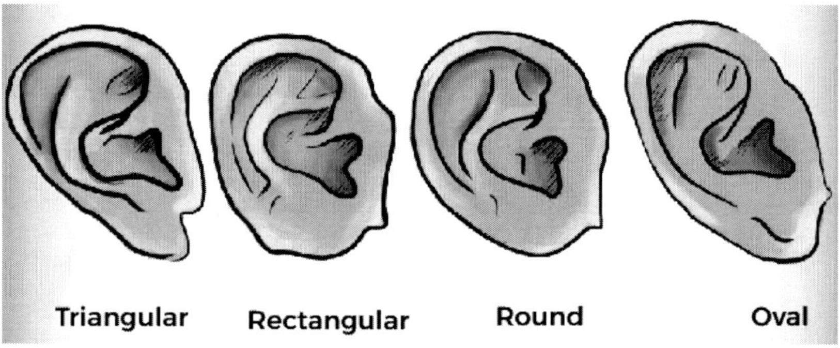

Figure 2. Various shapes of human auricle.

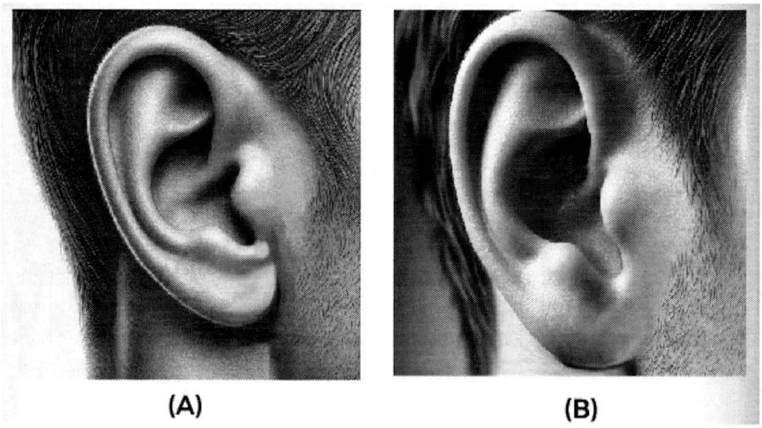

Figure 3. Earlobe conditions: free earlobe (A), Attached earlobe (B).

The earlobe is composed of connective tissue interspersed with fatty cells. There are two main types of earlobes in humans: attached and free earlobes (Figure 3). Studies have shown that the shape andattachment of the earlobes are hereditary traits, similar to the characteristics of other body organs. These studies, conducted over several generations, have concluded that certain features of the external ear can be effectively used in criminal identification (Attalla, et al., 2020).

Ear-Prints as a Biological Forensic Evidence

Biological evidence is at the forefront of forensic proof methods. It refers to evidence derived from body tissues and fluids such as blood, saliva, sweat, semen, vaginal secretions, urine, feces, and vomitus. Other body residues such as bones, hair and nails are also considered biological evidence. This category further includes body parts prints and impressions, such as fingerprints, lip prints, teeth prints and ear-prints. Additionally, remains associated with living organisms, particularly humans, such as plant residues, insects, pet hairs, or seeds, may also constitute biological traces that can be recovered from the scene of crime (Khalilia, and Rabaia, 2024). Ear-prints are classified as biological evidence and are among the most significant scientific proofs relied upon in criminal investigations. Their importance lies in their direct association with individuals involved in a criminal event, whether as criminals or victims (Naidu, et al, 2022).

Searching for Ear-Prints at the Crime Scene

An ear-print is the impress of the auricle recovered from various scenes of crime, typically in the form of latent prints. When burglars listen at the entrances and exits before breaking in to ensure no one is inside, they frequently unintentionally leave ear-prints at the scene (Krishan and Kanchan, 2025). Ear-prints can be discovered on several objects at crime scenes, including doors, windows, walls, car windows, and public payphones, where a suspect may have leaned in to listen, eavesdrop, spy, or look inside. In some cases, ear-prints may also be found on mobile phone screens, serving as valuable forensic evidence in a crime scene investigation. When a suspect or victim makes or receives a call, uses another person’s phone, is attacked while on a call, or listens to a recorded message, their ear-print could be deposited on the mobile screen. Although ear-prints are usually latent (invisible to the naked eye), they may they may sometimes appear partially or fully visible when stained with pigments, oils, or powders (Mustafa et al., 2020).

During a crime scene investigation, a systematic search plan must be followed by the experts or investigators to locate and preserve possible ear-prints. The process begins with identifying the crime location and determining the perpetrator's entry and exit routes. Investigators then trace the perpetrator's movements and examine all relevant objects, ensuring careful preservation to avoid contamination or destruction of evidence. When t ear-print is found, it is essential to verify that it belongs to the perpetrator rather than a resident or visitor. This involves collecting and comparing the ear-prints of all individuals who may have legitimate access to the premises with those found at the scene. The search for ear-prints are conducted using modern scientific techniques and tools, focusing on locations where the suspect's ear is most likely to have made contact such as doors, windows, walls, car windows, and public payphones. Upon discovering a potential print, the expert must carefully observe, document, and photograph it using appropriate forensic photography methods. Environmental factors such as air exposure, soil, or moisture can distort or degrade ear-prints, particularly when they are wiped or overlapped by new prints. However, if the ear-prints is in a closed, dust-free sene, the ear-prints will remain for a long period, ranging from two to three months, or even longer (Ahmad et al., 2024).

Collection and Preservation of Ear-Prints

Lifting prints is a technical procedure that should be carried out by a print expert or an investigator with sufficient expertise in print recovery. Several procedures for collecting ear-prints from suspects or directily from crime scenes have been described in the literature (Murgod, et al., 2013; Dash, and Vajpayee, 2021; Naidu et al. 2022).

Collecting Ear-Prints from Suspect

Ear-prints and fingerprints are generally collected using similar techniques. The prints can be visualized through physical or chemical method, depending on the nature of the surface and the condition of the print. Other techniques include photographing the ear-print, pressing the external ear against a flat glass surface to obtain standard impressions, and capturing thermographic images of the external ear. In addition, Three-dimensional (3D) samples can be obtained using dental detox resins, in which the resin is poured over a cotton plug and allowed to solidify to reproduce the 3D characteristics of the external ear (Kautilya, et al., 2013; Krishan, et al., 2019; Dash, and Vajpayee, 2021; Naidu et al. 2022).

Collecting Earmarks from the Crime Scene

Ear-prints at the crime scene may be either visible or latent, and the method of recovery depends on their condition and the surface on which they are located:

1. Visible Ear-Prints: When ear-prints are visible in any color, they can be lifted directly using appropriate type of plastic sheeting (white or black), according to the colour and type of the surface bearing the print. Photographing may be performed instead of, or in addition to, the lifting of the ear-prints using plastic sheeting. In cases where the substrate is lightweight or easily transportable, the entire object bearing the ear-print can be collected and sent to the forensic laboratory. This approach ensures better analytical conditions than those available at the crime scene. To prevent damage to the ear-print impressions, these items must be transported in special cardboard containers that prevent contact between surfaces. When the ear-print is visible, especially if it is bloody or formed in dust, it should be carefully photographed before any lifting is attempted, as brushing or contact during lifting may destroy or distort the print.
2. Latent Ear-Prints: When the ear-prints not visible to the naked eye, they must be developed using specialized forensic techniques. One common method involves the application of aluminum or white powder with a magnetic brush to reveal the invisible prints from dark colored objects, whereas black powder is used to develop prints on light-colored objects. The powder chosen should contrast with the color of the surface to ensure maximum visibility. To avoid damaging the delicate ridges and convolutions of the ear-print, the brush should always be moved in the same direction as the print pattern once its features become visible. After the ear-print has been developed and photographed, it is lifted carefully using a rubber lifter followed by a

transparent protective sheet to preserve it for further forensic examination.

1. In practice, powder is applied to a brush and lightly dusted over the surface suspected of containing ear-prints. The brush should be moved gently in a single direction across the surface until the ear-print features become visible, after which the brush is lifted carefully to prevent smudging or distortion. Any excess powder is then removed from the surface of the substrate, and the ear-print is lifted using the following procedure: *Powder selection and lifting medium:* When aluminum or white powder is used to develop ear-prints, they should be lifted using a black or transparent plastic strip. Conversely, when black powder is used, the prints should be lifted with white or transparent plastic tape to ensure adequate contrast.
2. *Application of adhesive tape:* Cut a piece of adhesive tape approximately matching the size of the ear-print, then carefully remove the clear backing from the tape and place it directly over the ear-print. Press the piece with one finger to ensure full adhesion to the surface, transfer the ear-print to the tape. Gently smooth out any air bubbles between the tape and the ear-print.
3. *Lifting and labeling:* Once adhesion is complete, lift the tape slowly from one side to transfer the ear-print. Reattach the original backing to protect the lifted print, and clearly label it with the case number, date, and investigator's initials for identification and chain of custody.
4. *Detection of aged or latent prints:* In the case of relatively old or faint ear-prints, iodine vapor is used to develop them. Specialized devices expose the print carrier directly to iodine vapor, and once the ear-print appears, it must be photographed immediately, as iodine impressions tend to fade quickly.
5. *Transportation and preservation:* After collection, the ear-print substrate or lifted sample should be securely packaged using specialized containers that maintain its integrity. Avoid using paper or cloth envelopes, as these materials can damage or obscure the impression during handling or transport. The evidence should be sent promptly to the forensic laboratory for examination under controlled conditions.

The Recognition of Ear-Prints

Currently, the ear-print analysis including detection, comparison, and identification, is conducted using 3D Ear Recognition System (ERS). This technique relies on local shape descriptors and the Iterative Closest Point (ICP) algorithm, which is used to reconstruct 3D models of surfaces taken from multiple scans. Recent studies have demonstrated the feasibility of extracting 3D ear features using 3D models captured using sequential video clips (Masaoud et al. 2013; Benzaoui, et al., 2023; Oyebiyi et al. 2023). Abdulghani and AL-Sulaifanie (2017) evaluated the ERS system to determine the optimal image segmentation regions that yield the highest recognition accuracy. Their findings showed that the proposed system achieved a first-class recognition rate of 93.75%, confirming the system's potential effectiveness in forensic ear-print identification.

Studies on Earmarks as an Individual Identification

Many researchers around the world have addressed the possibility of using the morphological variation of the external ear among humans for individual identification in criminal cases (Verma et al. 2014; Lai et al., 2017; Yadav, 2017; Petekkaya et al. 2020; Fakorede et al. 2021; Hassan et al., 2025). Previous studies have revealed significant differences in the morphological characteristics of the external ear across global populations, which explored anatomical variations in the ear between males and females, as well as alterations in external ear morphology over time (Brucker, et al. 2003; Sharma, et al. 2008; Kumar & Selvi, 2016; Laxmi et al., 2017; Kumar et al., 2021).

Cases in Which Ear-Prints Are Used as Criminal Evidence

The world is witnessing an increase in the prevalence, diversity, and complexity of crimes, including murder, burglary, robbery, rape, and others, many of which are challenging to solve. This has led to the necessity of developing advanced methods for crime detection, investigation, and offender identification. Although ear-prints are not as widely recognized as other forms of biological trace evidence, such as fingerprints or DNA, attempts to utilize them began through empirical observations and experimental studies many years ago. These efforts encouraged scientists to develop standardized models for measuring and comparing ear-prints, thus establishing a novel source of forensic evidence.

Since the mid-1960s, forensic investigators have employed ear-prints as part of criminal investigations. In one of the earliest documented cases, two earmarks were discovered among the traces of a 1965 burglary in Bienne, Switzerland. Hirschi (1970) was among the first to recognize their evidentiary value for individual identification. Two suspects were later arrested for a separate burglary, and tool mark evidence linked both incidents. A connection between the two burglary instances was established by tool mark evidence. The two males who were caught had their ear-prints collected so that they could be compared to the marks found at the Bienne scene. However, one of the two male's reference prints was different. The other's prints exhibited a remarkable resemblance to those foundat the crime scene. Hirschi consequently concluded that the latter suspect had participated in the Bienne burglary (Meijerman, et al., 2005).

A notable murder case occurred in Osaka, Japan, in 1985, involving a member of the Yakuza who murdered his business partner following a dispute. During the struggle, the victim's ear-prints were transferred onto glossy paper. When the authorities confronted the accused with the charge, but upon searching his room, the victim's ear prints were found and matched. This evidence was confirmed by the testimony of the worker who installed the glossy paper on the same day the victim was killed (Al-Maaytah, 2007). In other criminal case, David Wayne Kunze was charged with aggravated murder and other offences in Washington State (1996), where a latent ear-print constituted the main piece of evidence. The defense sought to exclude ear-print identification, prompting the court to convene expert witnesses, including forensic print examiners and otologists. The hearing concluded that ear-print identification had achieved general scientific acceptance, leading the court to admit the evidence (Meijerman et al, 2005).

Similarly, in Leeds Crown Court (1998), Mark Dallagher was convicted of murder based largely on ear-print evidence. Two expert witnesses testified that the defendant was the maker of the latent ear-print, either certain or very likely. In another case, Mark Kempster was convicted of seven counts of burglary and attempted burglary at Southampton Crown Court (2001). One of the main pieces of evidence against him was the unmistakable identification of an ear-print recovered from the scene of the crime as his. The appellate court ruled (2008) that the ear-print evidence was admissible and that the jury could use it to assess whether the appellant was the one who left the mark at the scene after he successfully challenged his conviction twice (Manikam et al. 2025). These cases collectively demonstrate that the use of the external ear for personal identification represents a modern and innovative advancement in forensic science and criminal investigation methodologies.

The Importance of Ear-Prints as Means of Forensic Proof

Ear-prints are one of the key types of biological impressions, and what most distinctly characterizes any biological print is its uniqueness to each individual. No two individuals share identical ear-prints, making them a valuable biometric marker. With the continuous advancement of forensic science for crime detection, and identification, offenders have, conversely, become increasingly adept at concealing or obliterating traces of their involvement. This has driven forensic experts to explore and adopt new evidentiary methods capable of identifying perpetrators even in the absence of traditional clues. Fingerprints have long been the cornerstone of personal identification in forensic practice. However, scientific research has not stopped there; however, scientific research has not stopped there; it has progressively evolved to include additional biometric identifiers that can provide comparable reliability and evidential value. These include lip prints, ear-prints, sweat prints, and voice prints, among others (Qanuna, 2020). From a practical perspective, ear-prints are particularly distinctive, as their morphological features differ not only between individuals but also between an individual's right and left ear. In forensic investigations, ear-prints are typically collected from surfaces where a suspect's ear has come into contact such as doors, windows, walls, luggage, or confined spaces—often during acts like eavesdropping or forced entry (Krishan and Kanchan, 2025). Consequently, ear-prints have become a valuable addition to the catalog of forensic evidence that may be relied upon for criminal identification when required (Krishan and Kanchan, 2025).

In criminal investigations, ear-prints can serve several forensic functions: they may exonerate an innocent person, provide corroborative evidence against a suspect, or be searched in databases when no suspect is yet known. Ear-prints recovered at a scene can confirm or refute a person's presence. They can also help identify a mobile phone user, and the shape and size of the ear may assist in reconstructing the offender's facial features in forensic investigations (Alexander et al., 2010). For these reasons, the importance of ear-prints as significant forensic evidence in front of the criminal court, as they may be a means to solving otherwise puzzling crimes (Singh and Pathak, 2013; Naidu et al. 2022).

If used optimally, ear-prints could rival or in some contexts even surpass other biometric methods such as fingerprints. Unlike fingerprints, ear impressions can sometimes be captured indirectly (for example, from surfaces or images) without detaining a suspect. However, treating ear-prints as biological traces presents practical challenges: they are difficult to locate at a scene, fragile during lifting and transport, and are relatively uncommon compared with other traces. Consequently, investigators should complement traditional recovery of biological ear-traces with advanced technological approaches. Today, ear-print analysis increasingly uses images captured by surveillance cameras at crime scenes. Although some offenders attempt to evade facial recognition by masking or concealing their faces, improvements in high-resolution imaging and image-processing techniques enable forensic analysts to extract and enhance ear images from surveillance footage. These images can then be used as reliable forensic evidence, expanding the opportunities to identify perpetrators when direct ear-prints from the scene are not available.

If a state collects high-resolution ear-prints from its citizens, it can maintain a comprehensive ear-print database. In the event of a crime, if forensic traces at the scene are deliberately concealed, nearby surveillance cameras can be used to track suspects. Their ear-prints can then be matched against the database, enabling authorities to identify the perpetrator.

Ear-prints are not only useful for identification but can also facilitate arrest. An electronic application is being developed for use with public surveillance systems, linked directly to national security authorities. The application is designed to track criminals through ear-print recognition, and if a match is detected, it automatically sends the suspect's location data to the relevant law enforcement agencies. Compared to facial recognition techniques, ear-prints can offer greater accuracy and, unlike other methods, do not necessarily require the suspect to be physically present in the justice system. Consequently, ear-prints provide a highly effective tool for identifying and apprehending criminals in such situations (Manikam et al., 2025).

Limitations of Ear-Prints as Means of Forensic Proof

As previously mentioned, Ear-prints serve as strong forensic evidence in criminal investigations. However, in practice, they have not received the same attention as other types of physical evidence, such as fingerprints. This can be attributed to several factors, including the difficulty of locating and collecting ear-prints due to their often unpredictable placement and lack of clarity. In many cases ear-prints may not be visible on flat surfaces at a crime scene, particularly when the external ear is obstructed by long hair, head coverings, or winter clothing. These barriers make it challenging to obtain usable impressions. Moreover, identifying the precise locations of ear-prints requires significant technical expertise, as such traces are often latent or concealed within the environment (Meijerman et al. 2005).

Despite the effectiveness of ear-print evidence in securing convictions, its forensic reliability remains a subject controversy. Concerns have been raised concerning its admissibility as a sole form of forensic evidence in the court. This is due to several factors that can affect the visibility, quality, and consistency of ear-prints, including the level of skin secretions, the texture of the surface, and variations in pressure applied during contact. Moreover, the absence of standardized forensic methodologies has resulted in divergent legal interpretations, with some courts deeming ear-print evidence inadmissible. Nevertheless, several forensic scientists worldwide have successfully employed ear-print analysis in criminal investigations, particularly in burglary cases, demonstrating its potential value in practice (Manikam, et al. 2025).

Although recent advances in ear-prints analysis have emerged across various countries, accurate quantitative assessment remains underdeveloped. In many regions, the necessary modern equipment, analytical tools, and standardized protocols are still limited or unavailable. Additionally, perpetrators often leave ear-prints in public areas before committing a crime, and the exact time of print formation cannot be determined, which further complicates their forensic use.

Conclusion

This chapter emphasized the significance of ear-prints as biological forensic evidence that can assist in solving certain types of crimes, particularly burglaries. It also outlined the key anatomical characteristics of the human external ear, which can be used to distinguish between individuals, and discussed the rationale for relying on ear prints as physical evidence in criminal identification and case resolution Recently, ear-prints have been instrumental in solving numerous criminal cases worldwide, several of which are discussed in this chapter. Ear-prints at crime scenes, whether visible or latent, are typically located in areas, where a perpetrator has pressed their ear to listen or eavesdrop before entering a building, attempting to determine whether anyone is inside. Consequently, forensic experts must conduct a meticulous and systematic search to locate and recover such latent prints. This chapter also examined the procedures for handling ear-prints both at the crime scenes and later within forensic laboratories. Similar to fingerprints, ear-prints are photographed, lifted, and preserved by trained technicians before being transported for analysis, where they are examined using advanced scientific tools such as the 3D ERS. Despite these advancements, ear-prints have not yet achieved widespread acceptance among specialists compared to other established types of forensic evidence in many countries. This limited acceptance is primarily due to challenges in locating complete and usable ear-prints at crime scenes and the technical difficulties associated with their collection and analysis. The chapter concludes that ear-prints represent a valuable modern form of forensic biological evidence that can complement other identification methods in criminal investigations. However, further research and methodological standardization are needed to enhance their reliability and increase their acceptance within judicial systems.

References

Abdulghani, B. A., AL-Sulaifanie, A. K. (2017). Ear Recognition Using Local Binary Pattern. *Journal of Duhok University, 20(1),* 120-128. https://doi.org/10.26682/sjuod.2017.20.1.11.

Agrawal, M., Yadav, M., Harshey, A., Srivastava, A., & Yadav, V. K. (2023). A Study of External Ear Morphological Variation in Central Indian Population for Genealogical Purposes. *Arab Journal of Forensic Sciences & Forensic Medicine, 5(1),* 31-42. https://doi.org/10.26735/KEXU1412.

Ahmad, N. A., Nor, F. M., Shafie, M. S., Abdullah, N. K., Razak, N. A., Nor, N. U., and Omar, N. (2024). A study of ear biometrics in autopsied cases at the Universiti Kebangsaan Malaysia Medical Centre. *Egypt J Forensic Sci, 14 (5).* https://doi.org/10.1186/s41935-023-00374-x.

Alexander, K. S., Stott, D. J., Sivakumar, B., and Kang, N. (2010). A morphometric study of the human ear. *J Plast Reconstr Aesthet Surg., 64*, 41-7. https://doi.org/10.1016/j.bjps.2010.04.005.

Al-Maaytah, O. M. (2007). *Criminal Evidence* - First Edition - Dar Al-Thaqafa – Jordan, 101 and beyond.

ALzwae, M. (2019). Ear Prints and their impact as Criminal Evidence. *AJFSFM,* 1(9):1341. https://doi.org/10.26735/16586794.2019.020.

Andrea, R. (2016). Biometrics' new identity-measuring more physical and biological traits. *EMBO reports, 17(1),* 22-26. https://doi.org/10.15252/embr.201541677.

Attalla, S. M., Kumar, K. A., & Hussain, N. (2020). Study of the Ear Shape and the Lobule Attachment among the Adult Malaysian Population at Shah Alam. *European Journal of Molecular & Clinical Medicine, 7(3)*, 5417-5425.

Benzaoui, A., Khaldi, Y., Bouaouina, R., Amrouni, N., Alshazly, H., and Ouahabi, A. (2023). A Comprehensive survey on ear recognition: Databases, approaches, comparative analysis, and open challenges. *Neurocomputing, 537*, 236-270. https://doi.org/10.1016/j.neucom.2023.03.040.

Biwasaka, H., Usui, A., Takamiya, M., Angelakopoulos, N., Cameriere, R., Kumagai, A. (2024). Validation of morphological ear classification devised by principal component analysis using three-dimensional images for human identification. *PLoS ONE, 19(10)*, e0306843. https://doi.org/10.1371/journal.pone.0306843.

Brucker, M. J., Patel, J., & Sullivan, P. (2003). A morphometric study of the external ear: age- and sex-related differences. *Plastic and reconstructive surgery, 112(2)*, 647-52. https://doi.org/10.1097/01.PRS.0000070979.20679.1F.

Champod, C. (2009). *Ear-prints, Forensic Evidence* of. In: Li, S. Z., and Jain, A. (eds.) *Encyclopedia of Biometrics.* Springer, Boston, MA. https://doi.org/10.1007/978-0-387-73003-5_105.

Dash, H. R., Vajpayee, K. (2021). *Collection, Preservation, and Transportation of Biological Evidences*. In: Dash, H. R., Shrivastava, P., Lorente, J. A. (eds.) *Handbook of DNA Profiling*. Springer, Singapore. https://doi.org/10.1007/978-981-15-9364-2_3-1.

Deepak, A., Kumar, S. (2016). Anthropometric Measurements of External Ear. *Research Journal of Pharmacy and Technology, 9(9)*, 1379. https://doi.org/10.5958/0974-360X.2016.00264.X.

Fakorede, S. T., Adekoya, K. O., Fasakin, T. P., Odufisan, J. O., & Oboh, B. O. (2021). Ear morphology and morphometry as potential forensic tools for identification of the Hausa, Igbo and Yoruba populations of Nigeria. *Bulletin of the National Research Centre, 45*, 1-19.

Gupta, D., Chand, S., Chandan, D., Shah, D., Bhapkar A., and Kulkarni, V. (2023). "EarSiamNet: Leveraging Siamese Networks and SVM for Ear Biometric Authentication," *2023 International Conference on Modeling, Simulation & Intelligent Computing (MoSICom)*, Dubai, United Arab Emirates, 2023, pp. 570-575, https://doi.org/10.1109/MoSICom59118.2023.10458801.

Hassan, K. K., Ali, S. M., & Saleem, R. I. (2025). Phenotypic variations of the human ear in the Basrah population. *Otolaryngologia polska = The Polish otolaryngology, 79(2),* 1-7. https://doi.org/10.5604/01.3001.0055.0000.

Kaushal, N., and Kaushal, P. (2011). Human ear-prints. *Journal of Biometrics & Biostatistics, 2(5),* 1-5. https://doi.org/10.4172/2155-6180.1000129.

Kautilya, D. V., Badkha, P., Poothanathan, P. (2013). Determination of stature and sex from anthropometry of the foot among South Indians. *International Journal of Review in Life sciences, 3(2)*, 22- 26.

Khalilia, W. M., and Rabaia, A. M. (2024). Level of Experiences in Processing of Biological Forensic Traces at the Crime Scene among Palestinian Police Employees. *J Forensic Investigation.11 (1),* 1.

Krishan, K., and Kanchan, T. (2025). *Ear Marks and Controversies*, Editor(s): Jason Payne-James, Roger W. Byard, Encyclopedia of Forensic and Legal Medicine (Third Edition), Elsevier, 394-402. https://doi.org/10.1016/B978-0-443-21441-7.00337-X.

Krishan, K., Kanchan, T., Thakur, S. (2019). A study of morphological variations of the human ear for its applications in personal identification. *Egyptian Journal of Forensic Sciences 9(6),* 1-11. https://doi.org/10.1186/s41935-019-0111-0.

Kumar, B. S., & Selvi, G. P. (2016). Morphometry of ear pinna in sex determination. *International Journal of Approximate Reasoning*, 4, 2480-2484.

Kumar, R., Maheshwari, S., Singh, H. P., & Kumari, P. (2021). Anthropometric measurements of auricle in population of Uttar Pradesh. *International Journal of Scientific Research, 10(10),* 53-55. https://doi.org/10.36106/ijsr.

Lai, P. S., Osman, K., Ismail, N. A. (2017). A Preliminary Study on Earprint Identification among Young Adults in Malaysia. *J of Forensic Sci & criminology, 2348-9804.* https://doi.org/10.15744/2348-9804.5.201.

Laxmi, V., Palak, Nidhi, S., Kullar, J., & Sharma, R. (2017). External ear: morphological and morphometric study in north Indian males and females. *International Journal of Approximate Reasoning, 5*: 3866-3869.

Manikam, V., Rajamanickam, R., Dahlan, N. K., & Dahlan, N. K. (2025). Importance and Reliability of Ear Print Analysis as Evidence. *Journal of Posthumanism, 5(3),* 296–304. https://doi.org/10.63332/joph.v5i3.736.

Marinkovic, S. and Valjarevic, S. (2014). The Auricle in Anatomy, Evolution, Anthropology and Art. *Journal of Otology & Rhinology, 03(02).* https://doi.org/10.4172/2324-8785.1000152.

Masaoud, A. K. S. Khairuddin, O., Md Jan, N. (2013). 3-Dimensional ear recognition based iterative closest point with stochastic clustering matching. *Journal of Computer Science, 10(3)*, 477-483. https://doi.org/10.3844/jcssp.2014.477.483.

Meijerman, L., Sholl, S., Conti, F. D., Giacon, M., Lugt, C. V. D., et al. (2004). Exploratory study on classification and individualization of ear-prints. *Forensic Sci Int., 140,* 91-9. https://doi.org/10.1016/j.forsciint.2003.10.024.

Meijerman, L., Thean, A., Maat, G. J. R. (2005). Ear-prints in forensic investigations, *Forensic Sci Med Pathol., 1*, 247-56. https://doi.org/10.1385/FSMP:1:4:247.

Murgod, V., Angadi, Hallikerimath, S., Kale, A. (2013). Anthropometric study of external ear and its applicability in sex identification: assessed in an Indian sample. *Australian J Forensic Sci., 45(4),* 431-444.

Mustafa, R., Chyad, H., George, D. (2020). Human Ear Print Detection Algorithm. *International Journal of Engineering Research and Advanced Technology (IJERAT), 6*, 2454-6135. https://doi.org/10.31695/IJERAT.2020.3644.

Naidu, R., Ravi Chander, D., & Aishwarya, M. (2022). Analysis of the morphological features of ears in human identification– a forensic study. *Journal of Population Therapeutics and Clinical Pharmacology,* 29(04), 1021-1025. https://doi.org/10.53555/jptcp.v29i04.3662.

Oyebiyi, O. G., Abayomi-Alli, A., Arogundade, O. 'T., Qazi, A., Imoize, A. L., & Awotunde, J. B. (2023). A Systematic Literature Review on Human Ear Biometrics: Approaches, Algorithms, and Trend in the Last Decade. *Information, 14(3),* 192. https://doi.org/10.3390/info14030192.

Petekkaya, E., Özandaç Polat, S., Kabakcı, A. G., Çevik, Y. (2020). Assessment of ear metric properties in young Turkish adults. *J Surg Med., 4(8),* 698-701.

Qanuna, F. Z. (2020). Scientific Methods in Criminal Evidence - Master's Thesis - Faculty of Law and Political Science - Abdelhamid Ibn Badis University Mostaganem, 8.

Sforza, C., Grandi, G., Binelli, M., Tommasi, D. G., Rosati, R., et al. (2009) Age-and sex-related changes in the normal human ear. *Forensic Sci Int., 187*, 110. https://doi.org/10.1016/j.forsciint.2009.02.019.

Sharma, A., Kumar, A., Singh, P. (2008). Age dependant changes in lobules of human ear and its influence on individual identification. *Ind J Forensic Med Toxicol. 2*, 1–3.

Singh, J., Pathak, R. K. (2013). Morphometric sexual dimorphism of human sternum in a north Indian autopsy sample: Sexing efficacy of different statistical techniques and methods: a comparison with other sexing methods. *Forensic Sci Int., 228*, 174.e1-174.e10.

Swift, B., Rutty, G. N. (2003). The human ear: its role in forensic practice. *J Forensic Sci., 48(1)*, 153-60. https://doi.org/10.1520/JFS2002251.

Verma, K., Bhawana, J., Vikas, K. (2014). Morphological Variation of ear for Individual Identification in Forensic Cases: A study of an Indian Population. *Res. J. Forensic Sci., 2(1)*, 1-8.

Verma, P., Sandhu, H. K., Verma, K. G., Goyal, S., Sudan, M., & Ladgotra, A. (2016). Morphological Variations and Biometrics of Ear: An Aid to Personal Identification. *Journal of clinical and diagnostic research, 10 (5),* ZC138-42.

Wang, B., Dong, Y., Zhao, Y., Bai, S., Wu, G. (2010). Computed tomography measurement of the auricle in Han population of north China. *J Plast Reconstr Aesthetic Surg., 64*, 34-40. https://doi.org/10.1016/j.bjps.2010.03.053.

Yadav, M. M. (2017). A Preliminary Study on Frequency Distribution & Inheritance Pattern of Different Characteristics of Ear among Population of Moth Region of Jhansi District. *International Journal for Research in Applied Science and Engineering Technology*, 236-241. https://doi.org/10.22214/ijraset.2017.10037.

Zhang, H. S., Chen, S. J., Zeng, H. C., Xiong, H., Lin, J. F., Xu, Y. D., Zhao, H. Y., Zheng, Y. Q. (2020). Characteristics of 43 multiple auricular deformity case families and auricle morphology in 463 microtia patients in South China. *Ann Transl Med., 8(7),* 496. https://doi.org/10.21037/atm.2020.03.212.

Chapter 5

The Male Experience of Victimization: A Call for Gender-Inclusive Forensic Practices

Kaileigh M. Chretien*
Kayla M. Gaw
and Leke J. Adeleke
Integrated Forensic Program, Royal Ottawa Mental Health Center and Institute of Mental Health Research, Ottawa, Ontario, Canada

Abstract

Society often endorses certain perceptions about sexual victimization and who fits the criteria of a 'victim.' Such beliefs frequently invalidate male experiences of sexual violence, particularly when the perpetrator is a woman. Influenced by traditional gender roles, young boys who have been sexually abused by women are rarely recognized as victims and are often perceived as having participated in a consensual 'rite of passage' sexual encounter. Boys themselves are therefore more likely to perceive their abuse as acceptable or even positive. However, research has shown that sexual abuse perpetrated by women can result in significant trauma and negatively impact their victims' social, emotional, and sexual development. This chapter reviews existing literature that explores the phenomenon of male sexual trauma and its systemic invalidation, including minimization tactics often employed by legal and health professionals. It also emphasizes the negative effect that prevailing attitudes regarding gender, sexuality, and victimization have on male sexual and psychosocial development, examining relevant implications for sexual abuse intervention efforts.

---

* Corresponding Author's Email: kaileigh.chretien@gmail.com

In: Frontiers of Forensic Science: Innovation, Technology, and Justice
Editor: Walid M. Khalilia
ISBN: 979-8-90134-160-5

Keywords: sexual assault, review, male victims, PTSD, stigma, forensic science, reporting barriers, male victimization

Introduction

Literature on the subject of sexual assault has primarily focused on female victims and male perpetrators. However, emerging literature indicates that male victimization occurs more often than previously believed (Depraetere et al., 2020). Since the primariy focus has long centered around female victims, the victimization experiences of other genders and sexual minorities remain underexplored in the extant literature. This lack of research and understanding also stems from legal policies and societal perceptions of sexual assault that inadvertently exclude male victims (Depraetere et al., 2020). As a result, the sexual victimization of men is often under recognized and under reported due to male victims feeling invalidated and scrutinized through pervasive stereotypes (Depraetere et al., 2020). Common myths and stereotypes surrounding masculinity can result in male victims suffering in silence, contributing to long-term psychological effects such as post-traumatic stress disorder (PTSD), shame, depression and anxiety (Depraetere et al., 2020). Research also highlights a significant shortage of gender-neutral support resources, which can lead to male victims feeling isolated and unsupported in coping with the aftermath of sexual assault (Catton et al., 2023; Donne et al., 2018). This chapter examines factors which invalidate male sexual victimization by exploring common stereotypes and myths, as well as the limitations of appropriate legal recognition and service provisions. The chapter also explores the social and psychological barriers that prevent male victims from seeking and receiving adequate support, and the consequent effects these barriers have on their recovery and well-being.

Literature Review

Prevalence and Underreporting

Literature investigating the prevalence of male sexual victimization remains significantly understudied, which may be largely due to underreporting practices (Depraetere et al., 2020). Underreporting of sexual assault is a common occurrence among both male and female victims, and is often caused by the lack of support society provides to victims (Thomas & Kopel, 2023). Thomas and Kopel (2023) highlight that prior research consistently discusses how men are substantially less likely to report sexual assault. For instance, it is estimated that 90-95% of sexual violations against men go unreported (Thomas & Kopel, 2023). Stanek et al. (2023) highlight that according to the 2014 national Clery Act statistics, 32% of student campus crimes were sexual offences, yet only approximately 20% of sexual assaults involving students were reported. They further emphasize that the high level of unreported sexual offences is often driven by fear of retaliation from the perpetrator, feelings of guilt or shame, and uncertainty about whether the incident constitutes sexual assault. Overall, research on sexual victimization has primarily focused on female victims and the factors that deter reporting, leaving a substantial gap in understanding the prevalence and reporting behaviours of male victims.

Historically, narrative framing of sexual assault victimization positions females as the "ideal victim" and men as the perpetrators (Depraetere et al., 2020; Walfield, 2018). Consequently, many victim support services offered for victims of sexual assault are thus geared toward the needs of female victims and are often located in women's clinics (Depraetere et al., 2020). Although it is not contested that females are indeed sexually victimized at a higher rate than males, a comparison of prevalence rates across gender vary drastically when research deviates from narrow definitions that solely focus on penetrative acts. Depraetere et al. (2020) found that victimization (since the age of consent) to be 66.3% for males and 83.9% for females. They further observed that studies employing broader definitions of sexual assault tend to yield higher prevalence rates, while those using narrower criteria report lower figures (Depraetere et al., 2020; Walfield, 2018). Thomas and Kopel (2023) reference the definition of sexual victimization used by the Centres of Disease Control and Prevention (CDC), which defines it as "*a sexual act that is conducted or attempted by another person without the victim's freely given consent or against someone unable to consent or refuse*"(p.1). Thomas and Kopel (20230 noted that 'sexual assault', 'sexual harassment', 'non-penetrative sexual acts', 'attempted rape', and 'rape' are all classified as forms of violent sexual behaviours. When examining studies that adopt broader definitions instead of limiting the definitions to only include penetrative acts, Thomas and Kopel (2023) found that per the 2019 National Crime Victimization Survey, the percentage of violent victimization that had been reported to police 46% of the victims were female and 36% were male. Additionally, the survey reported that once simple assaults were excluded, victimization rates were similar across gender (47% female and 46% male)

(Thomas & Kopel, 2023). Similarly, a literature review by Houghton et al. (2023) found that approximately one in six men experience some form of sexual abuse in their lifetime, often occurring before the age of 18.

Inconsistencies in Defining Sexual Assault

A significant barrier that has historically deterred male victims from reporting sexual assault may be narrow legal definitions of sexual assault, which have often referenced females in their definition of victim (Peterson et al., 2011). Globally, many legal systems define rape and sexual assault in ways that exclude male victims, particularly in cases that involve non-penetrative sexual violence or female perpetrators (Depraetere et al., 2020). While several countries have adopted more gender-neutral legislation, many legal systems continue to define sexual assault and rape with language that explicitly excludes the experience of male victims (Depraetere et al., 2020; Peterson et al., 2011). Legal definitions of rape have been historically defined as penile to vaginal penetration without consent (Javaid, 2018, p. 106). This narrow legal framework effectively exclude male victimization, and reinforce the belief that sexual assault is a crime committed solely against women by men (Depraetere et al., 2020). Narrow legal definitions can also limit legal discourse and result in less severe judicial outcomes for female perpetrators, further invalidating the experience of male victims (Javaid et al., 2018).

Although there has been a push for gender-neutral legal definitions of sexual offences, the implementation of such legislation varies significantly across countries. Some regions have modernized their laws, although the reporting rates among male victims remain (Sexual Offences Act, 2021). low. For example, the Criminal Code of Canada (CCC) adopts broader language when defining sexual assault, encompassing any form of unwanted sexual activity, including touching, intercourse, or any other sexual contact without consent (Criminal Code, 1985, s. 271). In the CCC, the legislation does not classify rape as a separate sexual offence, unlike its United Kingdom (UK) Counterpart. In contrast, UK legislation classifies rape as a sexual offence that involves penile penetration of the vagina or anus, thereby implying that women cannot legally commit rape under this definition (Sexual Offences Act, 2021).

Some legal definitions, such as those in the UK, imply that women are incapable of committing the offence, and use language that may exclude males as victims of rape. These legal gaps may limit the ability of male victims to feel they can pursue justice, and thus discourage victims from taking legal action against their perpetrators (Depraetere et al., 2020; Walker et al., 2005). Furthermore, it is argued that the lack of gender sensitivity within legal processes and law enforcement responses contributes to lower prosecution rates and insufficient support for male victims throughout judicial proceedings (see Gaw & Gojer, 2026).

Common Stereotypes and How They Invalidate Male Victims

Literature on the sexual victimization of men remains limited compared to that which focuses on female victims (Bullock & Beckson, 2011). However, the academic space has seen a gradual increase in studies that include male victims of sexual victimization. Several studies highlight a range of gender stereotypes, myths, and sexual scripts that significantly shape societal and institutional perceptions of male victimization (Davis, 2023; Depraetere et al., 2020; Peterson et al., 2011; Thomas & Kopel, 2023).

Such myths include the idea that men are rarely assaulted and often bear responsibility for their assaults (Bullock & Beckson, 2011; Davis, 2023). Additionally, some believe that male victimization is rare or that it occurs only in prison settings (Depraetere et al., 2020; Thomas & Kopel, 2023). While it has been suggested that individuals in incarceration do face a heightened risk of sexual assault, Depraetere et al. (2020) explain how the narrow perception obscures the reality that male sexual victimization occurs in a wide range of contexts. Societal perceptions of masculinity suggest that men are physically dominant and always in control (Peterson et al., 2011). Such perceptions may lead to skepticism and disbelief regarding the occurrence of sexual assault or rape against men, as the notion of a man being overpowered and forced into a sexual encounter is often mocked and dismissed (Davis, 2023; Depraetere et al., 2020; Thomas & Kopel, 2023).

Another common myth is the belief that male ejaculation during an assault implies consent (Bullock & Beckson, 2011). Despite this widely held but inaccurate belief, studies have found that men can experience involuntary physiological reactions, such as an erection, during traumatic events, which should never be interpreted as evidence of consent (Walker et al., 2005). Studies indicate that, regardless of their mental state towards consent, men may experience biological responses such as involuntary erection when faced with stress, fear, or physical stimulation (Hlavka, 2017). Misunderstandings of male physiological reactions regarding male arousal and ejaculation during a sexual assault contribute to this myth and have caused disbelief towards male victims in both society and among victims themselves (Thomas & Kopel, 2023; Walker et al., 2005). Male victims might be met with invalidating questions, such as how they could achieve or maintain an erection during a non-consensual encounter (Thomas et al., 2023). These responses not only invalidate victims but also reinforce harmful misconceptions towards male victims. Contemporary research emphasizes that physiological responses are automatic bodily reactions and do not indicate consent, willingness, or pleasure (Hlavka, 2017; Thomas & Kopel, 2023). Such misconceptions can lead male victims to doubt their own experiences and cause victims to feel confused and ashamed of their interpretation of the assault (Depraetere et al., 2020).

Furthermore, the belief that men are less affected or traumatized than women who are sexually assaulted, and therefore do not experience psychological distress after being sexually victimized, is also commonly accepted (Depraetere et al., 2020). This misconception stems from deeply ingrained gender stereotypes suggesting that men are inherently less vulnerable to trauma than women are. Such stereotypes reinforce the notion that men's expressions of vulnerability are signs of weakness and are therefore perceived as "unmanly" (Depraetere et al.,2020).

In addition to the myths discussed above, a common stereotypical response highlighted in the literature is that reactions to male victims often depend heavily on the characteristics of the perpetrators. This is noted to be a result of the persistent misconception that women cannot be perpetrators (Thomas & Kopel, 2023). The literature indicates that disclosures from male victims involving female perpetrators are more likely to elicit negative or dismissive reactions compared to disclosures from other victims (Depraetere et al., 2020). Male victims who disclose that a woman perpetrated sexual abuse often have their experiences ignored, minimized or reframed through a lens of gendered expectations. Traditional gender roles have fostered the belief that males who are sexually abused by women are not true victims of abuse, but rather willing participants in a consensual or even 'rite of passage' sexual encounter (Weiss, 2010; Javaid, 2018). Societal narratives and media representations often sexualize such male encounters, portraying them as desirable or flattering, while undermining the seriousness of the sexual abuse and dismissing the victim's experience as flattering.

Victims who receive negative or invalidating messages in response to their disclosure frequently experience shame and fear of social stigma (Thomas & Kopel, 2023). Studies suggests that such shame may prompt victims to alter their perception of the event and attempt to restore their social image by internalizing and minimizing their emotions while blaming themselves for the assault (Catton et al., 2023; Thomas & Kopel, 2023). These stereotypes and myths substantially contribute to the invalidation of male victims, leading to underreporting, limited recognition, and insufficient support services for men who have been sexually victimized.

Barriers to Help-Seeking

Stereotypical beliefs surrounding what qualifies as sexual assault often led male victims to feel that their experiences do not align with the commonly accepted definition of the sexual assault (Catton et al., 2023; Depraetere et al., 2020). In addition to the stigma resulting from the stereotypes mentioned above, male victims of sexual assault frequently encounter societal stereotypes, stigma, and a lack of specialized support services designed to meet their needs (Donne et al., 2018). Availability of appropriate support services significantly impedes help-seeking behaviour among male victims, particularly when healthcare or legal professionals themselves hold stereotypical beliefs (Donne et al., 2018; Thomas & Kopel, 2023). These misconceptions and beliefs have reinforced the false notion that male victimization is less severe or less deserving of support, which has contributed to the scarcity of resources specifically developed for male victims (Donne et al., 2018). The lack of services, training, and informed policies creates substantial barriers to care and often leads to underdiagnosis and delayed treatment for the physical and psychological effects of sexual victimization (Depraetere et al., 2020; Javaid, 2018). The invalidation of male victims alters their understanding and interpretation of their experiences, which reinforces stigma and fosters feelings of shame and guilt (Catton et al., 2023). Societal perceptions regarding male victimization have led many men to believe that those from whom they seek support may disbelieve, ridicule, or minimize their accounts of sexual assault (Thomas & Kopel, 2023). Existing literature indicates that male victims often anticipate dismissive or skeptical reactions from police officers and healthcare professionals, which further discourages reporting and help seeking. Moreover, some victims may hold preconceived notions of what constitutes sexual assault and may fail to recognize their experiences as such if they do not align with traditional or widely accepted definitions of victimization (Thomas & Kopel, 2023).

Research suggests that some men utilize societal misconceptions about sexual assault as a coping mechanism, to downplaying their emotions and refraining from identifying as victims in an attempt to preserve their sense of masculinity or control (Thomas & Kopel, 2023). Additionally, Studies have found that male victims are less likely to report their assault if they experience discomfort discussing their sexuality, particularly when the perpetrator is another male (Thomas & Kopel, 2023). The stigma surrounding sexual orientation has been consistently highlighted in the literature as a significant barrier to help seeking. For heterosexual men who are sexually victimized by another male, the fear that their disclosure will lead others to question their sexuality often deters them from seeking support (Hlavka, 2017). In comparison, gay or bisexual men who are sexually victimized tend to be deterred from seeking support due to concerns of facing discrimination and being stereotyped, or secondary victimization (Hlavka, 2017). Furthermore, in environments where sexual violence is minimized and rarely acknowledged, such as correctional institutions, male victims are particularly deterred from seeking support (Depraetere et al., 2020; Thomas & Kopel, 2023). Within these environments, individuals who disclose victimization of sexual violence may worry about how it would impact their reputation, social standing or personal safety (Depraetere et al., 2020; Javaid, 2018).

The Impact of Sexual Assault on Male Victims

The impact of sexual violence has significant physiological and psychological effects on victims, regardless of gender. Literature suggests that despite the prevailing stereotypical belief that men are less affected by sexual assault, male victims may experience psychological effects that are as severe as, or more severe than, those experienced by female victims (Walker et al., 2005; Depraetere et al., 2020). It may be that men undergo heightened psychological distress when processing their trauma due to the additional stigma surrounding their victimization (Depraetere et al., 2020; Gaw et al., 2025). In cases where the perpetrator is a woman, the effects on male victims, though frequently dismissed, can cause significant trauma, especially in cases involving manipulation and exploitation of power dynamics (Weiss, 2010; Javaid, 2018). Research indicates that sexual abuse perpetrated by women can lead to severe psychological harm, leaving male victims with feelings of shame, confusion, and isolation due to fears about how society will perceive their experience (Davies & Rogers, 2006). Long-term effects of such victimization may include disruptions to sexual identity and functioning, impaired social development, difficulties with trust and intimacy, and distorted perceptions of consent (Easton et al., 2014).

Research suggests that the psychological effects experienced by male and female victims of sexual violence are largely comparable, with both groups reporting significant impacts such as Post Traumatic Stress Disorder (PTSD), substance abuse, suicidal ideation, and depression (Depraetere et al., 2020; Easton et al., 2014; Walker et al., 2005;). Among reported cases, male victims often meet the diagnostic criteria for PTSD, particularly when their experiences include a betrayal of trust, physical violence, or coercion (Easton et al., 2014). Symptoms of PTSD in male victims often include emotional numbness, nightmares, intrusive thoughts, and avoidance behaviours (Easton et al., 2014). Additionally, research has found that male victims commonly experience co-occurring issues such as anxiety, depression, substance abuse, and suicidal ideation (Depraetere et al., 2020; Walker et al., 2005). Moreover, young male victims have been found to experience higher levels of shame, anxiety, and PTSD compared to other groups (Depraetere et al., 2020; Dorahy & Clearwater, 2012). Male victims also frequently report feelings of isolation and a pervasive distrust of others, particularly in situations that are intimate or where they are emotionally vulnerable (Depraetere et al., 2020; Easton et al., 2014). Male victims may also withdraw from personal relationships (Easton et al., 2014). Consequently, male victims suffering from the psychological effects of sexual victimization often endure prolonged suffering and significantly delay disclosure, if they disclose at all (Depraetere et al., 2020).

Similar to female victims, male victims of sexual assault may also experience physical injuries during their assault (Duchesne et al., 2018). Sexual assault may also lead to disruptions to male victims' sexual functioning, such as erectile dysfunction, loss of sexual desire, and difficulties with intimacy (Duchesne et al., 2018). Research further indicates that some male victims may develop an aversion to sex or engage in compulsive sexual behaviours as coping mechanisms (Catton et al., 2023; Carlisle & Schmitz, 2023; Meston, 2006). An aversion to sexual activity following a sexual assault is often associated with avoidance of vulnerability or triggering memories as a way to "recoup" their sense of masculinity (Carlisle & Smith, 2023). Alternatively, victims who develop hyper sexuality as a coping mechanism may do so in an effort to regain control or to numb the emotional pain associated with their trauma (Meston et al., 2006). Overall, victims of sexual violence often struggle with trust and intimacy with others, which can reinforce feelings of isolation. Without addressing and receiving treatment and support, the psychological and physiological effects of sexual victimization may persist long-term, significantly diminishing quality of life (Thomas & Kopel, 2023.

Service Provisions and Legal Support

As previously mentioned, many medical facilities and services built to support victims of sexual violence have historically been designed with female victims in mind (Javaid, 2018). Although access to such services has slightly improved, the available support systems often fail to foster a sense of acceptance and inclusivity for male victims (Depraetere et al., 2020; Easton et al.,2014). This limitation has been attributed to the language used in awareness campaigns and intake sessions, which frequently focus on female victims and male perpetrators (Depraetere et al., 2020; Donne et al., 2018; Walker et al., 2005). Such gendered framing can make male victims feel unwelcome in these environments and discourage help-seeking behaviour. More recent literature has highlighted the need for improved training regarding male-specific trauma. This call for improvement stems from findings that services accessible to male victims are often met with awkward discomfort, disbelief and invalidating responses when victims attempt to disclose their experience to police officers or medical professionals (Depraetere et al., 2020; Weiss, 2010). Studies indicate that such reactions serve as a significant deterrents for male victims seeking help, underscoring the necessity for future training to be both trauma-informed and gender-inclusive (Depraetere et al., 2020).

Scholars have suggested that enhanced training should extend beyond medical professionals to include police officers and other legal professionals (Depraetere et al., 2020; Peterson et al., 2011). Recent research has also highlighted the importance of expanding outreach initiatives and services that cater specifically to male victims and discusses how some organizations have begun offering programs and therapy groups specifically for male victims. However, the availability of these services remains inconsistent and often underfunded (Depraetere et al., 2020). Further interest in research on the experiences of male victims of sexual assault has led to increased support to enhance advocacy aimed at challenging societal perceptions towards male victimization and reshaping previously accepted beliefs about gender and victimization. Additionally, literature stresses that more advocacy is required to ensure that all victims of sexual violence are included in outreach efforts, included in educational programs on sexual assault, and provided with stronger legal protections (Depraetere et al., 2020; Carlisle & Schmitz, 2023). Although awareness and acknowledgment of male victims have grown in recent years, persistent societal perceptions continue to hinder progress. Sustained advocacy and education are therefore necessary to promote legal reform and the development of inclusive, accessible support services for all victims of sexual violence.

Conclusion

The experiences of male victims have long been overshadowed and marginalized by cultural myths, societal norms, gendered stereotypes, and institutional neglect. These factors have influenced the justice system's treatment of male victims of sexual assault, contributing to the absence of comprehensive forensic frameworks that adequately recognize and address their needs. Stereotypes portraying men as always willing participants in sexual activity, immune to trauma, and invulnerable to victimization have perpetuated harmful narratives that invalidate and discourage male victims from seeking help. This chapter has demonstrated that such beliefs are not only inaccurate but are also profoundly damaging and reinforce systemic practices that overlook male victimization within legal and clinical contexts. By investigating and discussing the barriers male victims face, this chapter underscores the need for gender-inclusive forensic and clinical practices that validate and support the experiences of all victims. It is essential to recognize that acknowledging male victimization does not diminish the experiences of female victims; rather, it broadens the understanding of the diverse realities faced by all survivors of sexual violence. It is imperative that forensic professionals, law enforcement, medical professionals, and other support services receive specialized training and resources to respond to every case without bias or reliance on stereotypes. As research continues to investigate and dismantle the myths and stereotypes surrounding male victims of sexual assault, institutions must prioritize inclusive policies and evidence-based interventions that demonstrate a genuine commitment to equity and compassion in victim care.

References

Brooks, Carolyn, Stephanie Martin, Lisa Broda, and Jennifer Poudrier. 2017. "'How Many Silences Are There?' Men's Experience of Victimization in Intimate Partner Relationships." *Journal of Interpersonal Violence* 35 (23–24): 5390–5413. https://doi.org/10.1177/0886260517719905.

Carlisle, Zachary T., and Rachel M. Schmitz. 2023. "I Am a Man. How Could I Possibly Have Been Raped?" Men Making Sense of Their Experiences with Sexual Violence.'" *Journal of Interpersonal Violence* 38 (19–20): 10514–41. https://doi.org/10.1177/08862605231174500.

Catton, Ashley K., Martin J. Dorahy, and Kumar Yogeeswaran. 2023. "Disclosure of Sexual Victimization: Effects of Invalidation and Shame on Re-Disclosure." *Journal of Interpersonal Violence* 38 (13–14): 8332–56. https://doi.org/10.1177/08862605231155122.

Davies, Michelle, and Paul Rogers. 2006a. "Perceptions of Male Victims in Depicted Sexual Assaults: A Review of the Literature." *Aggression and Violent Behavior* 11 (4): 367–77. https://doi.org/10.1016/j.avb.2006.01.002.

Davies, Michelle, and Paul Rogers. 2006b. "Perceptions of Male Victims in Depicted Sexual Assaults: A Review of the Literature." *Aggression and Violent Behavior* 11 (4): 367–77. https://doi.org/10.1016/j.avb.2006.01.002.

Davis, Gianna E. 2023. "Reacting to Non-Prototypical Victims: Blame, Empathy, and Willingness to Label Sexual Assaults of Men and Sexual Minority Victims." *Journal of Interpersonal Violence* 38 (11–12): 7457–84. https://doi.org/10.1177/08862605221145709.

Depraetere, Joke, Christophe Vandeviver, Tom Vander Beken, and Ines Keygnaert. 2020. "Big Boys Don't Cry: A Critical Interpretive Synthesis of Male Sexual Victimization." *Trauma, Violence, & amp; Abuse* 21 (5): 991–1010. https://doi.org/10.1177/1524838018816979.

Donne, Martina Delle, Joseph DeLuca, Pavel Pleskach, Christopher Bromson, Marcus P. Mosley, Edward T. Perez, Shibin G. Mathews, Rob Stephenson, and Victoria Frye. 2018. "Barriers to and Facilitators of Help-Seeking Behavior among Men Who Experience Sexual Violence." *American Journal of Men's Health* 12 (2): 189–201. https://doi.org/10.1177/1557988317740665.

Dorahy, Martin J., and Ken Clearwater. 2012. "Shame and Guilt in Men Exposed to Childhood Sexual Abuse: A Qualitative Investigation." *Journal of Child Sexual Abuse* 21 (2): 155–75. https://doi.org/10.1080/10538712.2012.659803.

Duchesne, Sophie, Marie Seyller, and Patrick Chariot. 2018. "Male Sexual Assaults in the Paris, France Area: An Observational Study over 8 Years." *Forensic Science International* 290 (September): 16–28. https://doi.org/10.1016/j.forsciint.2018.06.018.

Easton, Scott D., Leia Y. Saltzman, and Danny G. Willis. 2014. "'Would You Tell under Circumstances like That?': Barriers to Disclosure of Child Sexual Abuse for Men." *Psychology of Men & amp; Masculinity* 15 (4): 460–69. https://doi.org/10.1037/a0034223.

Hlavka, Heather R. 2017. "Speaking of Stigma and the Silence of Shame." *Men and Masculinities* 20 (4): 482–505. https://doi.org/10.1177/1097184x16652656.

Houghton, Aimée W., Lesley Nicole Knight, and Rachel Joseph. 2023. "Male Sexual Abuse." *Journal of Pediatric Surgical Nursing* 12 (4): 119–25. https://doi.org/10.1097/jps.0000000000000371.

Gaw, K. M., & Gojer, J. A. (2026). Female sexual violence: differential sentencing, paternalism, and implications for research. Psychology, Crime & Law, 1-13.

Javaid, Aliraza. 2018. "Male Rape, Masculinities, and Sexualities." *International Journal of Law, Crime, and Justice* 52: 199–210. https://doi.org/10.1007/978-3-319-52639-3.

Meston, Cindy M., Alessandra H. Rellini, and Julia R. Heiman. 2006. "Women's History of Sexual Abuse, Their Sexuality, and Sexual Self-Schemas." *Journal of Consulting and Clinical Psychology* 74 (2): 229–36. https://doi.org/10.1037/0022-006x.74.2.229.

Peterson, Zoë D., Emily K. Voller, Melissa A. Polusny, and Maureen Murdoch. 2011. "Prevalence and Consequences of Adult Sexual Assault of Men: Review of Empirical Findings and State of the Literature." *Clinical Psychology Review* 31 (1): 1–24. https://doi.org/10.1016/j.cpr.2010.08.006.

"Rape and Sexual Offences - Chapter 7: Key Legislation and Offences." 2021. Rape and Sexual Offences - Chapter 7: Key Legislation and Offences | The Crown Prosecution Service. May 21, 2021. https://www.cps.gov.uk/legal-guidance/rape-and-sexual-offences-chapter-7-key-legislation-and-offences.

Stanek, K. A., Fox, K. A., Telep, C. W., & Trinkner, R. 2023. "Who can you trust? The impact of procedural justice, trust, and police officer sex on women's sexual assault victimization reporting likelihood." *Violence against women 29* (5): 860-881.

Thomas, John C., and Jonathan Kopel. 2023. "Male Victims of Sexual Assault: A Review of the Literature." *Behavioral Sciences* 13 (4): 304. https://doi.org/10.3390/bs13040304.

Walfield, Scott M. 2018. "'Men Cannot Be Raped': Correlates of Male Rape Myth Acceptance." *Journal of Interpersonal Violence* 36 (13–14): 6391–6417. https://doi.org/10.1177/0886260518817777.

Walker, Jayne, John Archer, and Michelle Davies. 2005. "Effects of Rape on Men: A Descriptive Analysis." *Archives of Sexual Behavior* 34 (1): 69–80. https://doi.org/10.1007/s10508-005-1001-0.

Weiss, Karen G. 2010. "Male Sexual Victimization." *Men and Masculinities* 12 (3): 275–98. https://doi.org/10.1177/1097184x08322632.

Chapter 6

Forensic Spectroscopic Analysis: Modern Technologies and Practical Applications

Walid M. Khalilia[1,*]
and Kamel N. Aljoundi[2]
[1]Department of Forensic Science, Al-Istiqlal University, Jericho, Palestine
[2]Department of Criminal Research and Investigation, Faculty of Graduate Studies and Scientific Research, Al-Istiqlal University, Jericho, Palestine

Abstract

Forensic science has undergone transformative advancements with the incorporation of spectroscopic analysis, which provides fast, accurate, and often non-destructive methods for examining physical evidence both at crime scenes and forensic laboratories. These techniques operate by analyzing how different materials interact with electromagnetic radiation, producing unique spectroscopic "signatures" that can help distinguish forensic traces such as drugs, explosives, bodily fluids, fibers, and other types of forensic evidence. A wide range of methods fall under this umbrella, including infrared (IR) spectroscopy, ultraviolet-visible (UV-Vis) spectroscopy, Raman spectroscopy (RS), mass spectrometry (MS), nuclear magnetic resonance (NMR) spectroscopy, hyperspectral imaging (HSI), spectroscopic fluorescence imaging (SFI), and X-ray spectroscopy. Each technique offers distinct advantages: some are portable and suitable for field use, while others provide highly detailed molecular information. However, these technologies are not without challenges. Environmental interference, high equipment costs, and the need for specialized training factors can hinder widespread adoption. Consequently, standardized testing protocols and controlled laboratory

* Corresponding Author's Email: walidkhalilia@pass.ps

In: Frontiers of Forensic Science: Innovation, Technology, and Justice
Editor: Walid M. Khalilia
ISBN: 979-8-90134-160-5

conditions are essential to ensure the accuracy and legal reliability of the results. The promising aspect is that advances in spectroscopic technology such as the development of portable devices and the integration of Artificial Intelligence (AI) for data interpretation, are making these spectroscopic analysis increasingly practical and accessible. This chapter explores the key principles of these spectroscopic techniques, their real-world forensic applications, the current limitations, andthe future prospects for their role in criminal investigations.

Keywords: forensic spectroscopy, crime scene investigation, infrared spectroscopy, raman spectroscopy, mass spectrometry, hyperspectral imaging, nuclear magnetic resonance spectroscopy, artificial intelligence

Introduction

Forensic science has progressed significantly with the integration of modern analytical technologies, transforming traditional investigative procedures into more precise and systematic approaches. Among these innovations, forensic spectroscopic analysis stands out as one of the most impactful tools, enabling experts to examine the chemical and physical properties of forensic traces without causing damage. Spectroscopic techniques operate by analyzing how materials interact with electromagnetic radiation, producing distinctive patterns "spectral fingerprints" that allow for the accurate identification and classification of substances discovered at crime scenes. This capability has made spectroscopy an essential component of modern forensic investigation and solving crimes. Forensic spectroscopic analysis is involves the collection, comparison and interpretation of data obtained from physical evidence using advanced spectroscopy instruments. It is particularly effective in detecting and analyzing forensic traces such as fibers, paint fragments, bodily fluids, and chemical residues. These insights gained through these analyses assist investigators reconstructing events and establishing scientifically validated evidence that can be presented in court in an admissible and reliable form (Chen et al., 2009; Rosenblatt, et al., 2019). Scenes of crime often contain complex mixtures of trace materials, including chemical drugs, biological fluids, explosives residues, fibers, and other forms of physical evidence. Traditional analytical methods such as microscopic examinations and spot chemical tests, often lack the sensitivity and specificity needed to analyze and identify such mixed samples effectively. In contrast, spectroscopic techniques have emerged as powerful alternatives, offering rapid, precise, and sometimes field-deployable detection capabilities that have significantly advanced forensic research and investigation. These techniques include Infrared (IR) spectroscopy, Raman Spectroscopy (RS), Mass Spectrometry (MS), Nuclear Magnetic Resonance (NMR), Ultraviolet-Visible (UV-Vis), and X-ray spectroscopy, as well as modern imaging approaches such as Hyperspectral Imaging (HSI) and Spectroscopic Fluorescence Imaging (SFI). Each of these methods contributes unique analytical strengths, enabling forensic scientists to identify, differentiate, and characterize substances with high reliability (Lim & Lewis, 2013; Wei et al., 2016). The fundamental principle of forensic spectroscopy lies in the concept that every physical substance interacts with light in its own unique manner by absorbing, scattering, or emitting electromagnetic radiation. These interactions produce distinct spectral patterns often referred to as a compound's molecular identity or spectral fingerprint for each substance. Forensic scientists analyze these spectral signatures and compare them against reference databases established from verified standards to accurately identify unknown substances. Because most spectroscopic techniques are non-destructive, multiple analyses can often be performed on the same piece of evidence using different methods. This enhances the credibility, reproducibility, and legal admissibility of the forensic findings presented in court (Lim & Lewis, 2013; Ewing & Kasparian, 2017).

Forensic spectroscopic analysis has played a key role in modernizing crime scene investigations, enabling the real-time identification of substances without damaging or compromising the evidence. Portable spectroscopic devices such as Fourier Transform Infrared (FTIR) and Raman spectrometers, have become indispensable in the field, allowing investigators to directly examine drugs, biological traces, fibers and other materials at the scene. These instruments are not only compact and user-friendly but also highly sensitive, capable of detecting subtle molecular variations that are critical for distinguishing between visually similar substances. Furthermore, the integration of advanced technologies such as HSI and UV-Vis spectroscopy has significantly broadened forensic capabilities, enabling the detection of bloodstains, Gunshot Residue (GSR), or documents alterations even under challenging environmental conditions. Collectively, these innovations provide immediate, on-site analytical insights, reducing reliance on delayed laboratory analyses and enhancing the accuracy, efficiency, and evidential reliability of forensic investigations (Brandenburg et al., 2021; Mariota et al., 2023; Ganapati et al., 2025).

The process of forensic spectroscopic analysis typically follows several key stages, including evidence collection, data acquisition, preprocessing, analysis, interpretation, and reporting (Figure 1). During the collection phase, samples must be handled meticulously to prevent contamination, degradation, or loss of trace material. Instruments such as RS, MS, and IR spectrometers are then employed to capture the distinct molecular signatures of the evidence. Once the raw spectral data is gathered, they undergo preprocessing and computational analysis using advanced methods such as chemo metrics and pattern recognition, which help extract meaningful features from complex datasets. These analytical steps are vital for transforming raw spectroscopic signals into reliable, interpretable results that can support forensic conclusions with scientific precision. The interpretation phase focuses on identifying substances, determining their origins, and establishing possible connections between the evidence, suspects, and crime scenes. AI and machine learning algorithms are being integrated into this workflow to enhance detection sensitivity and specificity, particularly for mixed or degraded samples. The final phase involves compiling the analytical outcomes into a comprehensive forensic report suitable for legal and judicial use. Maintaining sample integrity and data quality throughout all stages remains fundamental to maintaining the credibility and admissibility of spectroscopic evidence (Boven et al., 2019).

Figure 1. Phases of spectroscopic analysis workflow.

However, forensic spectroscopic analysis faces several challenges, such as environmental factors including humidity, lighting, and surface irregularities, which can degrade data quality (Bruce et al., 2024). Additionally, the high cost of instruments and the need for specialized operators have limited its widespread adoption, particularly in resource-limited settings (Lewis, et al., 2024). Current studies aim to develop portable multi-technique spectrometers, integrate Artificial Intelligence (AI) for automated data interpretation, and develop standardized protocols to overcome these obstacles (López-López, et al., 2023; Zhou, et al., 2024). This chapter presents a thorough overview of forensic spectroscopic analysis, highlighting its fundamental principles, key techniques, and applications in criminal investigations. It explores the use of advanced technologies such as IR, RS, MS, HSI, UV-Vis, NMR and SFI. This chapter also discusses the use of AI in interpreting large and complex datasets resulting from these spectroscopic techniques. Furthermore, it addresses technical and practical implementation challenges and discusses the future trajectory of the field, emphasizing the growing importance of spectroscopic tools in delivering accurate and legally sound forensic evidence.

Major Spectroscopic Techniques Used in Forensic science

Spectroscopic analysis is one of the most advanced and practical techniques in modern forensic science, offering accurate and non-destructive methods to examine criminal evidence both at crime scenes in laboratory settings. It is particularly valuable because it allows for the identification and analysis of compounds without altering or damaging the sample, thereby preserving the integrity of forensic traces. Recent years have witnessed remarkable progress in this field through the combination of cutting-edge imaging technology and spectroscopic systems. Techniques such as IR, RS, MS, HSI, UV-Vis, and NMR spectroscopy have significantly enhanced the forensic identification of a variety of evidence, including biological fluids, latent fingerprints, fibers, drugs, explosives, etc.

Infrared (IR) Spectroscopy

By measuring the absorption of IR light at particular wavelengths, IR spectroscopy determine the chemical structures and composition of different compounds. This method is widely applied in criminal investigations to examine chemical and physical evidence such as narcotics, explosives, Ballistics, and synthetic fibers without degrading and altering the evidence. IR spectroscopy provides crucial information about the functional groups found in compounds, making it an invaluable tool for forensic identification and material characterization (Ewing & Kasparian, 2017; Mokari et al, 2023).

FTIR spectroscopy is a widely utilized analytical method in forensic science that measures the absorption of infrared radiation by chemical substances to generate distinctive molecular spectra for their identification. This technique enables rapid and accurate characterization of a wide range of forensic materials, including solids, liquids, and fibers. A significant advancement within this method is Attenuated Total Reflectance Fourier Transform Infrared (ATR-FTIR) spectroscopy, which allows direct analysis of evidence samples without extensive preparation or destructive processing. ATR-FTIR enhances efficiency and reliability in forensic examinations, making it particularly valuable for the analysis of trace materials collected from crime scenes (Alkhuder, 2022).

ATR-FTIR spectroscopy is a commonly employed analytical instrument in forensic research due to its ability to perform surface-level chemical analysis, minimum sample preparation requirements, and non-destructive operation. This technique generates diagnostic spectra by measuring the absorption of IR light by chemical bonds, thereby revealing the functional groups and overall molecular composition of the examined materials. In the ATR configuration, the sample is placed in direct contact between the sample and an internal reflection element typically made of diamond, which allows for the rapid examination of solids and liquids. This makes ATR-FTIR particularly valuable in forensic scenarios where sample contamination must be avoided or where limited evidence is available for testing (Alkhuder, 2022).

ATR-FTIR is a highly valuable technique in forensic applications for the characterization trace evidence at crime scenes, including fibers, polymers, paints, stains, and bone residues. For instance, controlled experiments on polypropylene subjected to environmental weathering have demonstrated that ATR-FTIR can monitor oxidative changes, offering information on the ageing of the material and its exposure date that is relevant to the reconstruction of crime scenes (Anshari, et al., 2025).

Recent advances in ATR-FTIR imaging expanded its applications in forensic science. Systems based on focal plane arrays now enable the creation of spatially resolved chemical maps that differentiate between layered or heterogeneous materials. This capability facilitates detailed comparisons of paint chips, polymer blends, or localized residues on diverse substrates frequently encountered in forensic casework (Ewing & Kasparian, 2017). Within forensic labs, ATR-FTIR has become indispensable tool for material identification and comparison because it provides quick, repeatable, and surface sensitive molecular information while preserving the integrity of the evidence (Alkhuder, 2022).

ATR-FTIR is particularly valuable for distinguishing bodily fluids including blood, semen, and saliva. These fluid stains exhibit distinct absorption patterns, such as the amide I and II bands of proteins, which enable species classification, age estimation of stain, and discrimination from visually similar substances. Research demonstrates that ATR-FTIR, when paired with chemo metric models such as Principal Component Analysis (PCA) and Partial Least Squares Discriminant Analysis (PLS-DA) can accurately identify blood types and distinguish between menstrual and peripheral blood across various surfaces (Orphanou, et al., 2015; Takamura, et al., 2018; Sharma & Singh, 2020). FTIR is extensively utilized in textile and synthetic fibers analysis. A research conducted by Aljannahi et al. (2022) used ATR-FTIR integrated with PCA and Soft Independent Modeling of Class Analogy (SIMCA)to classify 138 synthetic fibers with approximately 97 % accuracy, underscoring its value in linking suspects to crime scenes through trace evidence (Aljannahi et al., 2022). Additionally, the technique has proven effective in cosmetic and adhesive trace identification. For example, ATR-FTIR analysis of red lipsticks on different substrates achieved over 99 percentage accuracy in brand discrimination using PLS-DA models (Ka Khei, et al., 2023). While ATR-FTIR coupled with chemo metric analysis has also been applied successfully to electrical tape identification in forensic investigations (Chongtham, et al., 2022).

In conclusion, FTIR spectroscopy is a cornerstone of modern criminal labs, offering a rapid, non-destructive, and highly accurate method of analyzing a range of forensic traces such as bodily fluids, fibers, cosmetics and adhesives. When combined with ATR and chemo metric techniques, it enhances analytical precision and interpretive reliability, reinforcing its indispensable role in contemporary forensic science.

Raman Spectroscopy (RS)

RS operates based on the inelastic scattering of monochromatic light, which produces information on structural details and molecular vibrations unique to each sample. Its non-destructive nature makes it highly suitable for forensic applications, allowing investigators to analyze stains, residues, and biological fluids directly at the scene or even through transparent containers without altering the evidence. (Suzuki, & Buzzing, 2018; George, et al., 2022).

RS is a powerful vibrational spectrum analysis technique that measures the inelastic scattering of monochromatic light to produce distinctive molecular-level fingerprints. In forensic science, RS is particularly valuable for the analyzing and identifying evidence such as drugs, stains, explosives, and trace materials including fibers and biological fluids. Its non-destructive nature and minimal sample preparation requirements make it ideal for preserving evidence integrity while providing accurate and reproducible analysis. RS has proven effective in the identification of biological samples, residues, and unknown powders, supporting reliable forensic interpretations (Chalmers, et al., 2012; Gardiner, 2013).

Bloodstain age estimation is one notable forensic application of RS. Doty et al. (2016), demonstrated that hemoglobin degradation-related changes detected by RS might be used to determine the age of bloodstains, which aid in scene of crime reconstruction. By utilizing metallic Nano-structures to rise signal sensitivity, Surface-Enhanced-RS (SE-RS) enabling the detection of forensic evidence such as dyes, drugs, and explosives at incredibly low concentrations. RS also shows significant potential for the analysis pen inks in contested documents and is helpful for trace comparison and linking investigations (Hakonen et al., 2018; Khandasammy et al., 2018; Souza et al., 2025). In high-risk or hazardous situations, RS enables non-contact evidence detection form several meter away, maintaining crime scene integrity. According to Almehmadi & Lednev (2024), RS allows for highly accurate and interference-free remote bloodstain detection. Furthermore, the analysis of complex spectroscopic datasets is made possible by the combination of deep learning and AI with RS. AI-driven models as developed by Bhattacharya et al. (2022) enhance specificity by reducing false positives and more accurately distinguishing between chemically similar substances. A controlled experiment was designed to evaluate the sensitivity of RS in identifying chemical residues on textile fibers demonstrating the technique's applicability in forensic investigation. Figure 2 illustrates the conceptual workflow of this experiment, encompassing all critical stages from defining from defining the research objectives to collecting, analyzing, and disseminating the data.

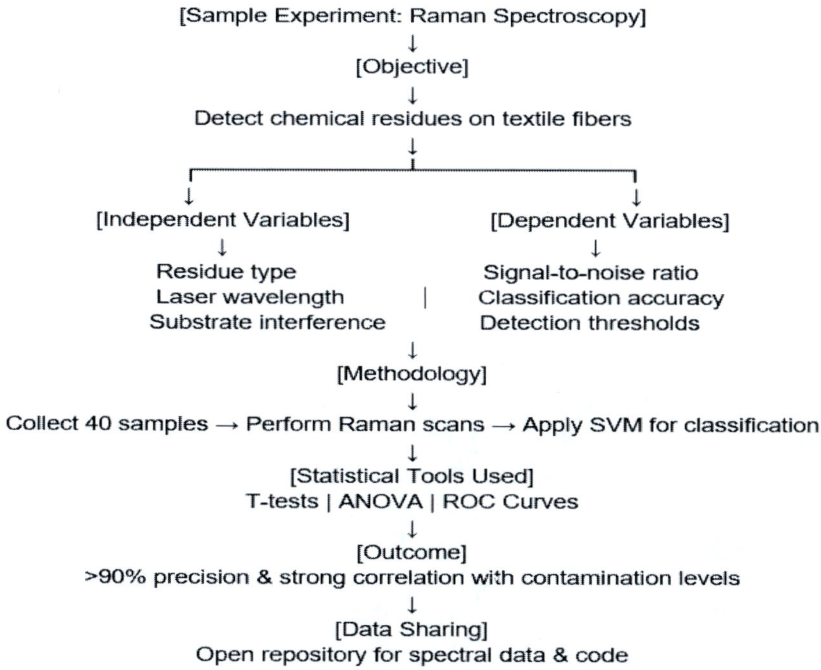

Figure 2. Conceptual design of a RS experiment for trace residue detection on fibers.

One of the objectives of this chapter was to assess the detection capabilities of handheld RS devices for low concentrations of chemical residues on various textile kinds. The researchers examined several variables, including the type of chemical utilized, the laser wavelength, and potential interference from the fabric. Silva et al., (2025), assessed the system's ability to reliability detect the minimal concentration, the clarity of the RS signal, and its accuracy in identifying residues. Their methodology involved collecting 40 textile pieces, each polluted to varying degrees, and scanning them with RS under standardized testing conditions. The resulting data were analyzed using machine learning, particularly Support Vector Machines (SVMs), to classify and identify the chemical residues. The effectiveness of this approach was validated using statistical methods such as ROC curves, ANOVA, and T-tests. The results demonstrated accuracy levels exceeding 90%, indicating a strong correlation between the RS signals and the degree of contamination (Tsai & Yuan, 2025).

In conclusion, RS including traditional RS, Surface-Enhanced RS (SERS), standoff RS, and AI-enhanced approaches represents a versatile, rapid, and highly sensitive tool for modern forensic research and investigations.

Mass Spectrometry (MS)

MS measures the mass-to-charge ratio (m/z) of ionized molecules, offering exceptional sensitivity and precision sensitivity. It is frequently used in criminal laboratories for the detection of narcotics, hazardous chemicals, and other important molecules, as it can accurately identify trace amounts of compounds in complicated combinations (Salazar Mogollón, et al., 2018). With its unmatched sensitivity, specificity, and quantitative accuracy in identifying a broad spectrum of chemicals in intricate matrices, MS is considered the gold standard analytical technique in forensic science. By ionizing chemical compounds and separating the resulting ions based on their m/z values, MS enables reliable molecular identification, even in challenging forensic cases involving biological fluids, drugs, explosives, and other trace evidence (Harper et al., 2017; Jackson & Barkett, 2023).

Drug detection in biological fluids represents a crucial forensic application of MS. Rapid drug and metabolite screening in whole blood and dried bloodstains is made enabled by techniques such as Liquid Chromatography–MS (LC–MS) and Paper Spray MS (PS-MS). To demonstrate the technique's efficacy in forensic toxicology, researchers developed PS-MS approach for monitoring antipsychotic medications in body fluids (Saar et al., 2010; Proença et al., 2020).

Additionally, ambient ionization techniques like Direct Analysis in Real Time–MS (DART-MS) allow for the rapid detection of explosives, drugs, or counterfeit medications directly at crime scenes, without the need for complex sample preparation (Ifa et al., 2009; Pavlovich et al., 2018; Sisco & Forbes, 2021). In forensic toxicology, MS provides higher specificity and accuracy than traditional immunoassays or urine tests. Comparative studies indicate that LC-MS/MS outperforms these conventional methods for detecting chemicals in body fluids (Kahl et al., 2019). Moreover, applications such as dried blood spot (DBS) demonstrate the ability to measure several medications using minimal sample volumes, while preserving stability under a range of storage conditions (Sadler Simões et al., 2018; Lee et al., 2023).

In conclusion, the combination of sophisticated MS techniques such as ambient ionization, LC–MS, PS-MS, and DART-MS provides forensic experts with the quick, precise, and high-throughput analytical skills, making them indispensable tools in modern crime scene investigations.

Hyperspectral Imaging (HSI)

HSI and multispectral imaging integrate high-resolution photography and spectroscopy to capture detailed spatial information along with the full spectrum of light across a broad wavelength range. In forensic investigations, this technology enables the non-destructive examination of materials and evidence directly at crime scenes. It can reveal latent fingerprints, bloodstains, drugs, document forgeries, and other critical traces, uncovering details often invisible to the naked eye (Smith et al., 2018; Mariota et al., 2023). HSI is a powerful forensic tool that combines imaging and spectroscopy to collect detailed information across a broad range of the electromagnetic spectrum. Unlike standard cameras, which only record visible light, HSI captures hundreds of spectral bands for every pixel. This capability allows forensic investigators to identify chemical compositions, subtle surface changes, and hidden evidence that would otherwise go unnoticed (Edelman et al., 2012). Its capabilities are especially valuable for detecting bloodstains even when they are faint, old, diluted, or obscured by the surrounding factors. Research has shown that HSI can distinguish blood apart from visually similar substances, such as rust or red wine, by analyzing their unique spectral fingerprints. This enables to reconstruct crime scenes more accurately and document evidence without physical contact or alteration (Cadd et al., 2016; Zulfiqar et al., 2021). HSI is also proven to be highly valuable in document examination. By detecting subtle spectral differences in ink, it can uncover alterations, added signatures, or forged sections even when the inks appear identical to the naked eye (Taylor et al., 2023). This capability makes it particularly effective for detecting modifications or overwrites in questioned documents (Silva et al., 2014). Beyond paper based evidence, HSI can analyze fibers, GSR, and paint samples without causing any damage, thereby assisting forensic scientists in distinguishing between that shares similar colors but differ in chemical compositions (Edelman et al., 2012; Głomb et al., 2018). Recent advances in portable HSI systems now enable investigators to perform such analysis directly at crime scene, accelerating decision-making and minimizing the need for extensive laboratory processing. Moreover, with AI increasingly integrated into forensic labs, the combination HSI data and machine learning techniques is enhancing pattern recognition and classification accuracy, particularly for small or trace evidence (Głomb et al., 2018; Mariota et al., 2023). In conclusion, HSI remains a powerful tool in forensic research and investigation, providing fast, nondestructive, and highly accurate analysis of various types of forensic traces. It thereby enhances the effectiveness of forensic investigations and ensuring the reliability of collected materials in criminal proceedings.

UV–Visible Spectroscopy

UV–Vis spectroscopy is a long-standing tool in forensics, used to identify and quantify substances based on their absorption ultraviolet and visible light. UV–Vis spectroscopy operates on the principle that different molecules absorb light at specific wavelengths, producing a unique spectrum that can be used to characterize or match forensic traces (Sharma et al., 2019; Wolstenholme, 2021). One of its key application in forensics is the examination of body fluids such as semen, bloodstains, and saliva. These fluids contain chromophores (light-absorbing components) that register in the UV or visible range, making them detectable on a variety of surfaces. As highlighted in a review by Bazyar (2023), UV–Vis spectroscopy plays an important role in the early detection of biological stains. It offers a non-destructive approach, which is particularly valuable at crime scenes where preserving the integrity of forensic evidence is critical (Bazyar, 2023).

UV–Vis spectroscopy also plays a crucial role in the examination of inks and dyes in questioned document analysis. By detecting subtle variations in spectral patterns, it can compare ink formulations to help verify authenticity, identify alterations, or distinguish between inks that appear visually identical. Using micro spectrophotometers, forensic investigators can analyze minute portions of handwriting or printing without causing any physical damage to the document (Adam, 2008). The technique is also valuable in forensic drug analysis, particularly for screening colored compounds or making preliminary assessment of drug classes in seized materials. While more advanced methods are typically required for confirmation, UV–Vis provides a rapid, cost-effective initial step in the analytical process (Kirkbride, 2000). In conclusion, the UV–Vis spectroscopy remains a versatile and essential tool in forensics, offering rapid, non-invasive analysis of a wide range of trace evidence at crime scenes, with significant utility in field and laboratory settings.

Nuclear Magnetic Resonance (NMR) Spectroscopy

NMR spectroscopy is a highly precise analytical technique that exploits the magnetic properties of atomic nuclei to provide detailed structural and quantitative information about molecules. In forensic science, it is valued for its non-destructive nature and for its ability to analyze complex mixtures with minimal sample preparation, making it particularly useful in forensic toxicology, drug profiling, and metabolomics investigations (Hussain, 2021). Recent advances in high-field magnets and cryoprobe technology have boosted NMR's sensitivity and expanded its forensic applications. Although the instrumentation is costly and requires specialized expertise, NMR's exceptional specificity, reproducibility, and ability to analyze small sample volumes make it a powerful complement to mass spectrometry in modern criminal labs.

One of its major roles in forensics is the identification of synthetic drugs and poisons. Through NMR-based metabolomics, investigators can track biochemical changes in biological fluids such as blood or urine after drug use or poisoning. This approach enables differentiation between various drug classes and even detect novel psychoactive substances without the need for reference standards. It has proven particularly reliable in cases of organophosphorus pesticide poisoning, which are frequently encountered in both intentional and accidental death investigations. NMR also excels in quantitative accuracy, assisting forensic chemists determine the concentration of active compounds in seized drugs or biological samples. In forensic pathology, NMR can be used to assess postmortem redistribution by analyzing chemical shifts and signal intensities in autopsy specimens, providing crucial insights into the time and cause of death (Koskela, 2010; Antonides et al., 2019; Szeremeta et al., 2021).

Spectroscopic Fluorescence Imaging (SFI)

SFI has become an increasingly important tool in forensics, valued for its non-destructive nature and high sensitivity in detecting both biological and chemical forensic traces. The technique operates by exciting target substances with specific wavelengths of light, causing them to emit fluorescence that can be captured and analyzed to obtain precise spatial and spectral information. This capability makes SFI particularly useful for examining evidence such as latent fingerprints, body fluids, and GSRs. SFI has demonstrated strong effectiveness in visualizing GSR on different surfaces. These particles, which are often composed of lead, barium, and antimony, can produce distinct fluorescent signals when illuminated under controlled conditions, allowing analysts to detect and localize GSR even in challenging crime scene environments or after significant time has passed since a shooting (Weber et al., 2014; Arouca et al., 2017). This technique is also widely employed to enhance the visibility of latent fingerprints and biological stains without causing any surface damage. When combined with fluorescent powders or dyes, SFI provides improved contrast and finer detail under alternate light sources. This approach has been successfully applied in both lab-based analyses and on-site forensic investigations (Lian et al., 2020; Boonyaras et al., 2023).

Beyond detecting traces, SFI has been incorporated into automated systems for scanning and documenting forensic evidence, enabling faster and more reliable screening about forensic traces at scene of crime. Research conducted at the University of Lausanne has also demonstrated that fluorescence techniques can be seamlessly integrated into forensic protocols, working effectively with modern imaging platforms and analytical software (Tsaklakidis et al., 2024).

X-Ray Spectroscopy

X-ray spectroscopy techniques provide detailed elemental and structural information about compounds, making them essential tools in modern forensic investigations and research. Two widely used methods are X-ray Fluorescence (XRF) and X-ray Diffraction (XRD). XRF enables rapid, non-destructive analysis of the elemental composition of materials such as glass fragments, paints, GSR, metals, and soils without consuming any of sample material, making it particularly valuable for source attribution and comparison. XRD, on the other hand, identifies crystalline phases in unknown powders or residues, adding another layer of precision to material characterization during forensic examinations. Advances in portable XRF devices have enabled on-site analyses, preserving evidence integrity while supporting timely decision-making and interpretation. Together, XRF and XRD significantly enhance the forensic investigation of diverse trace evidence types, offering both compositional and structural insights (Thatcher & Briner, 1986; Chen et al., 2015).

Other Spectroscopic Technologies

In addition to the spectroscopic methods discussed above, other advanced spectroscopic technologies are also employed in the analysis of forensic traces at crime scenes and in forensic laboratories, such as Laser-Induced Breakdown Spectroscopy (LIBS) and Atomic Absorption Spectroscopy (AAS). These are highly efficient spectroscopic techniques used in forensic science that offer rapid, sensitive, and minimally destructive elemental analysis. LIBS provides exceptional discrimination power for applications such as document analysis and glass fragment comparison, enabling rapid, in situ profiling of materials including glass, inks, metals, GSR, and soils with minimal sample preparation (El-Deftar et al., 2014). On the other hand, AAS enables precise quantification of heavy metals including arsenic, lead, and mercury and is widely used in forensic labs for quantitative determination of metals in biological samples, GSR, and toxicological investigations involving poisoning cases (Ferreira et al., 2019).

Comparative Effectiveness of Spectroscopic Techniques in Forensic Science

After reviewing the major spectrometric techniques used in forensic science, it becomes clear that each method possesses distinct characteristics and applications. Table 1 summarizes the key differences among RS, FTIR, MS, and HIS spectroscopic technologies, in terms of their principal forensic uses, as well as their respective advantages and limitations. Figure (3) provides a visual comparison of these techniques illustrating their strengths, weaknesses, and forensic applications.

In forensic science, all four analytical methods (Table 1) have a diverse applications and are essential for identifying and analyzing narcotics, biological fluids, explosives, fibers, and other trace evidence. Depending on the sample's characteristics and the level of sensitivity required, each approach offers distinct advantages for forensic investigations. For non-destructive analysis, RS, FTIR, and HSI are particularly beneficial, as they preserve evidence for future experimentation or presentation in court. These methods are often preferred in many preliminary studies due to their ability to analyze a wide range of components without altering the trace.

Table 1. Comparative of major spectroscopic technologies used in forensic science

Spec. Tech.*	Applications	Advantages	Limitations	References
RS	• Identifying drugs, biological fluids, explosives, and pigments. • Used in crime scene investigations and forensic toxicology. • Bloodstain dating and fingerprint analysis.	• Non-destructive analysis of trace evidence. • Can detect both organic and inorganic substances. • Ideal for on-site analysis with portable systems. • Can analyze samples through transparent containers.	• Limited sensitivity for certain compounds. • Requires specialized equipment and expertise. • Cannot always differentiate similar substances if spectra overlap.	Chalmers et al., 2012; Doty et al., 2016; Suzuki, & Buzzing, 2018; George et al., 2022; Almehmadi & Lednev, 2024; Souza et al., 2025
FTIR	• Characterizing body fluids (blood, semen, saliva). • Identifying drugs, explosives, and synthetic fibers. • Trace evidence analysis such as paints, plastics, and adhesives.	• Highly effective in identifying functional groups in molecules. • Fast and non-destructive. • Can analyze solid, liquid, and gaseous samples.	• Lower resolution compared to Raman for some applications. • Surface-sensitive and may not penetrate deeper layers. • Less effective for highly complex mixtures.	Chen et al., 2009; Ewing & Kasparian, 2017; Alkhuder, 2022; Ka Khei et al., 2023; Anshari, et al., 2025
HIS	• Detecting blood stains, fingerprints, and document alterations. • Identifying fibers and paint evidence. • Real-time analysis in crime scene investigations.	• Combines both spectroscopic and spatial information. • Can detect latent evidence invisible to the naked eye. • Non-destructive with a broad range of applications.	• Requires sophisticated equipment and processing time. • Expensive and less accessible for field use. • Requires advanced software for data interpretation.	Edelman et al., 2012; Głomb et al., 2018; Zulfiqar et al., 2021; Mariota et al., 2023

Spec. Tech.*	Applications	Advantages	Limitations	References
MS	• Drug detection, toxicology, and forensic chemistry. • Identifying narcotics, accelerants, explosives, and poisons. • Crucial for drug profiling and forensic toxicology.	• Unmatched sensitivity for detecting trace amounts of substances. • Highly specific and quantitative. • Suitable for complex samples like biological fluids and drugs.	• High cost and requires specialized operators. • Sample preparation can be labor-intensive. • High operational costs and maintenance.	Ifa et al., 2009; Harper et al., 2017; Kahl et al., 2019; Proença et al., 2020; Sisco & Forbes, 2021; Jackson & Barkett, 2023; Lee et al., 2023

* Spectroscopic Techniques.

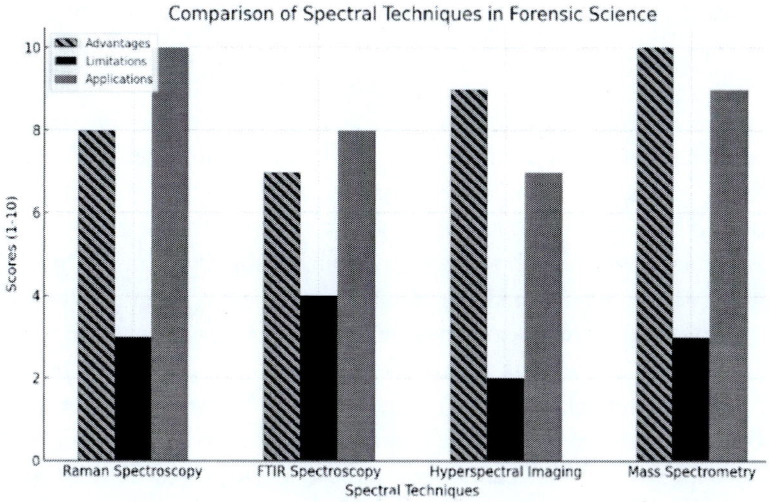

Figure 3. Molecular Spectroscopic Comparison Chart.

Because of its exceptional sensitivity and specificity, MS is a valuable technique for chemical and toxicological analysis. Nevertheless, it has several disadvantages including high cost, operational complexity, and demanding maintenance requirements (Figure 3). By bridging the gap between imaging and spectroscopy, HSI enables the visualization of latent evidence and the spatial distribution of materials. Despite its strengths, HSI remains limited by field usability, data complexity, and expense. Although on-site analysis is supported by portable RS and FTIR instruments, the size, cost, and need for specialized personal make both HSI and MS less suitable for field applications. Their routine use at crime scenes is therefore limited. RS excels in fieldwork and non-destructive analysis of trace evidence, while FTIR is more versatile for analyzing functional groups but may lack the spectral resolution of RS. HSI is particularly valuable in crime scene investigations, especially for detecting latent traces, but requires advanced equipment. MS stands out for its unmatched sensitivity, particularly when analyzing complex mixtures such as drugs and biological fluids (Mariota et al., 2023; Anshari, et al., 2025). Overall, a more comprehensive forensic investigation can be achieved by combining different techniques, as no single method is universally superior. Integrating these approaches enhances the reliability of forensic evidence interpretation.

Controlled Experimentation in Forensic Spectroscopic Analysis

Controlled experimentation is essential for validating spectroscopic techniques in forensics, particularly when evaluating their performance under simulated crime scene conditions. Through carefully designed trials, forensic analysts can assess the reliability, sensitivity, and specificity of methods such as FTIR and HSI. For instance, hyperspectral cameras can be used to examine various surfaces, such as fabric, paper, or skin, deliberately contaminated with biological or chemical residues. This process helps identify the unique spectroscopic signatures associated with each substance, ensuring that the technologies produce consistent and accurate results across a range of realistic scenarios (Edelman et al., 2012). Spectroscopic imaging also enables the precise localization and chemical mapping of trace evidence, such as body fluids or explosive residues, even when these are invisible to the naked eye. This capability not only confirms the presence of the evidence but also illustrates its distribution across a surface. Such experimental setups are critical for meeting regulatory and accreditation requirements, ensuring that instruments comply with forensic standards and generate results that are admissible in court. Moreover, by refining algorithms and calibration methods during these trials, spectroscopic techniques continue to advance in both accuracy and forensic reliability. The Experimentation in Forensic Spectroscopic Analysis – Conceptual Model (ExperFS-CM), adapted from the digital forensics (DF) field by OliveiraJr et al., (2020), provides a systematic framework for conducting and documenting forensic spectroscopy experiments (Figure 3). The model outlines five key phases:

1. *Planning:* Establishing the experiment's objectives and hypothesis, select appropriate instruments such as RS, FTIR, or MS, identifying key variables, and define evaluation criteria.
2. *Pre-Operation:* Preparing and calibrating the spectrometers, selecting suitable sample sets, and recreating crime scene conditions relevant to the investigation.
3. *Operation:* Carrying out the spectroscopic measurements under controlled conditions to maintain consistency, reproducibility, and reliability.
4. *Analysis & Interpretation:* Using chemometric methods, such as PCA or LDA along with appropriate statistical tests, to interpret and validate the acquired spectroscopic data.
5. *Dissemination:* Sharing the experimental design, results, and raw data to promote transparency, reproducibility, and peer evaluation within the forensic science community. As shown in Figure 4, each of these phases is interconnected with the central DF experiment, forming a structured framework that supports replication and transparent reporting, both of which are essential for achieving forensic validation.

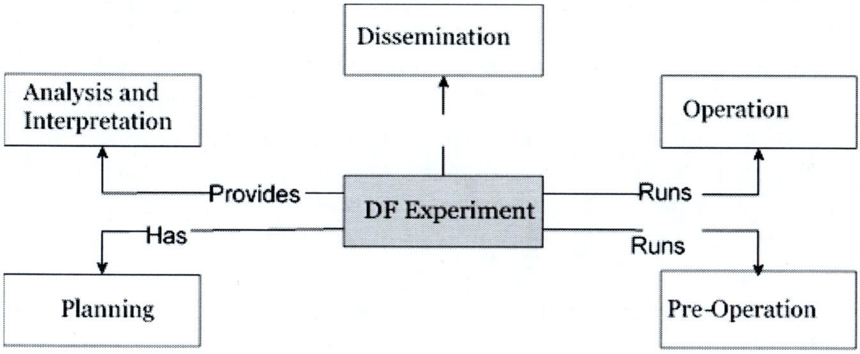

Figure 4. A visual overview of the ExperFS-CM model, showing how the different phases of forensic spectroscopic experiments connect and interact with the core DF experiment. Adapted from OliveiraJr et al. (2020).

Advancing Controlled Experimentation in Forensic Spectroscopy: Tools, Standards, and AI Integration for Legal Admissibility

As forensic science continues to integrate advanced spectroscopic technologies, it is increasingly essential to carry out controlled experiments that ensure the validity, consistency, and courtroom admissibility of results. Recent studies emphasize the growing need for standardized protocols, unified terminologies, and open-access databases to support rigorously designed forensic experiments using techniques such as RS, FTIR, and LIBS spectroscopy (Ntziouni et al., 2022; Gatta et al., 2023). The emergence of portable spectroscopic devices, coupled with AI and cloud-based data systems, has further enhanced the ability to collect reliable, high-quality data even in field settings (Huang & Yu, 2021). Moving forward, maintaining a careful balance between adopting innovative technologies and upholding strict methodological standards will be crucial to ensuring that forensic spectroscopic evidence remains both scientifically robust and legally defensible. The following section outlines key steps that researchers and institutions can implement to strengthen controlled experimentation in forensic spectroscopy.

Support Tools

Progress in forensic spectroscopy relies heavily on the continuous advancement of software and hardware tools that facilitate every step of the experimental process. These tools encompass design templates, procedural checklists, and simulation systems capable of replicating realistic crime scene conditions. Automated data collection helps reduce human errors, while chemo metric and machine learning algorithms enhance pattern recognition and enable the interpretation of complex data. Visualization platforms further improve analytical transparency by presenting results in a clear and interpretable manner. Emerging technologies like blockchain are also being explored to ensure data integrity, traceability, and secure documentation throughout experimental workflows. Despite these advances, the field still faces challenges arising from the absence of standardized testing environments and the limited availability of realistic, validated datasets (Chango et al., 2024).

Embracing Openness

Applying open science principles is essential for advancing controlled experimentation in forensic spectroscopic analysis. By openly sharing raw data, experimental protocols, and analysis code, researchers enable independent verification of results, thereby enhancing the reliability and transparency of findings. Publishing detailed methodological descriptions further ensures that experiments can be accurately replicated, which is crucial for building confidence in forensic techniques used in court. Open-source software development promotes collaborative refinement of analytical tools, while preregistration of experimental designs helps mitigate bias by requiring researchers to commit to their hypotheses and methodologies in advance. Moreover, archiving data and research outputs in publicly accessible repositories ensures long-term availability, supporting continual validation and further development of spectroscopic methods (Albright & Scurich, 2024).

Artificial Intelligence and Machine Learning

AI and machine learning have become indispensable tools for enhancing the design, execution, and dissemination of forensic spectroscopic experiments. AI excels at processing large and complex datasets, identifying subtle patterns that may be overlooked by traditional approaches. During planning phase, AI can generate predictive models and optimize experimental parameters, improving both efficiency and reliability. Machine learning classifiers automate the interpretation of spectroscopic signals, improving the accuracy of material identification. Additionally, AI facilitates the creation of synthetic datasets that simulate real forensic samples, addressing data scarcity and variability issues. Explainable AI models provide transparency, a critical requirement for ensuring that forensic evidence is admissible in court. Combined with portable spectroscopic devices and real-time data acquisition, AI enhances pattern recognition, classification, and anomaly detection, making forensic spectroscopy more reproducible, scalable, and practical for real-world investigations (López-López et al., 2023; Zhou et al., 2024; Guo et al., 2025).

Boosting Rigor in Forensic Spectroscopic Experiments

To improve the quality and efficiency of controlled experimentation in forensic spectroscopy, the adoption of formal experimental design frameworks is essential. These frameworks encourage clear hypotheses, rigorous control of variables, and consistent methods. Adherence to international forensic standards ensures that results are legally admissible and scientifically robust. Quality assurance measures, such as careful data validation and thorough documentation, help keep experiments reliable and reproducible. Additionally, staying abreast of emerging technologies and evolving forensic challenges supports the continuous refinement of experimental practices. By integrating these strategies, forensic spectroscopic research becomes stronger, efficient, and capable of withstanding scrutiny in both legal and scientific settings (Ntziouni et al., 2022).

Challenges and Future Directions in Forensic Spectroscopic Experiments

Controlled experimentation in forensic spectroscopy continues to face several challenges that constrain its reliability and limit its full potential. A major challenge is the lack of standardized protocols or widely accepted methods for designing and conducting these experiments. Without a common framework, data collection, processing, and interpretation can vary significantly between labs, reducing reproducibility and undermining the legal admissibility of results. Moreover, the inherent complexity of spectroscopic data coupled with changes in environmental conditions at crime scenes makes it difficult to maintain solid experimental controls. Another significant challenge is the scarcity of comprehensive and realistic datasets that accurately represent forensic samples, which restricts the testing, validation, and benchmarking of new spectroscopic techniques. Sharing data is further complicated by privacy concerns and institutional rules, which limiting collaboration and slowing progress within the forensic community. Moreover, while new technologies like AI and machine learning offer promising opportunities for enhancing experimental design and data interpretation, they introduce new challenges related to transparency, interpretability, and legal admissibility, which must be carefully addressed to ensure their trustworthiness in court. Looking ahead, the field of forensic spectroscopy must prioritize the development of standardized frameworks, better simulation platforms, and shared data repositories to encourage transparency, collaboration and reproducibility. Collaboration across disciplines, bringing together forensic scientists, chemometricians, and data scientists will be essential to advance the field.

Key areas for further focus include the integration of multiple spectroscopic techniques, such as RS and NMR, with AI to enhance the speed, accuracy, and reliability of analyses. The development of compact and portable devices will facilitate on-site crime scene investigations, while AI-driven analysis of large spectral datasets can reduce human errors and accelerate data investigations. To ensure these advances are effective, consistent standards, rigorous validation across laboratories, and ongoing professional training are critical. Such measures will enable forensic practitioners to confidently apply these technologies and present scientifically sound findings in court.

Controlled experimentation remains critical to ensure forensic spectroscopy produces evidence that is scientifically robust, reproducible, and legally defensible. Insights from related forensic fields such as fingerprint analysis, demonstrate that high levels of repeatability (approximately 90%) and reproducibility (around 80%) are achievable, providing a benchmark for spectroscopic methods. To improve the quality of spectroscopic investigations, labs should adopt consistent reporting standards, carefully document every step, and use statistical tools to identify potential errors early. Adherence to quality management systems, such as ISO/IEC 17025, ensures uniform standards consistent across crime labs, while collaborative inter-lab studies allow assessment of method performance under diverse conditions. Additionally, the development of shared databases and openly accessible libraries of spectroscopic data would significantly improve transparency, reproducibility, and confidence in forensic spectroscopy (Ulery et al., 2012).

Conclusion

Recent improvements in spectroscopic techniques have significantly transformed forensic science research and investigations. These methods enable experts to analyze substances with high accuracy while keeping the evidence intact and undamaged. Spectroscopic tools such as FTIR, NMR, LIBS, RS, MS, HSI, UV–Vis, and SFI have proven indispensable for detecting and interpreting a wide range of forensic traces, including drugs, poisons, bodily fluids, gunshot residues, and other critical evidence. Importantly, these techniques are effective not only in laboratory settings but also in the field, providing real-time, on-site analysis that enhances the efficiency of criminal investigations. Looking forward, the future of forensic spectroscopy will likely focus on further technological advancements, integrating AI, and the development of faster and more efficient analytical methods. The combination of AI with portable devices promises to make forensic work more accessible, accurate, and reliable. However, for these tools to achieve their full potential, there must be greater standardization, collaboration among labs, and ongoing training for professionals. Improving controlled experimentation in forensic spectroscopy will require coordinated efforts, including the developing of common standards, open data sharing, advanced simulation platforms, AI integration, quality control measures, and adherence to legal guidelines. By embracing these steps, forensic science can strengthen the reliability, reproducibility, and judicial acceptability of spectroscopic evidence, ultimately contributing to a more effective and trustworthy justice system.

References

Adam, C. D., Sherratt, S. L., & Zholobenko, V. L. (2008). Classification and individualisation of black ballpoint pen inks using principal component analysis of UV-vis absorption spectra. *Forensic Science International,* 174(1), 16–25. https://doi.org/10.1016/j.forsciint.2007.02.029.

Albright, T. D., & Scurich, N. (2024). A call for open science in forensics. *Proceedings of the National Academy of Sciences of the United States of America,* 121(24), e2321809121. https://doi.org/10.1073/pnas.2321809121.

Aljannahi, A., Alblooshi, R. A., Alremeithi, R. H., Karamitsos, I., Ahli, N. A., Askar, A. M., Albastaki, I. M., Ahli, M. M., & Modak, S. (2022). *Forensic Analysis of Textile Synthetic Fibers Using a FT-IR Spectroscopy Approach. Molecules,* 27(13), 4281. https://doi.org/10.3390/molecules27134281.

Alkhuder, M. A., AlHetlani, E., Amin, M. O., Al Qalfas, M., Alzahrani, F. M., & Alshammari, A. (2022). Attenuated total reflection–Fourier transform infrared spectroscopy: A universal analytical technique with promising applications in forensic analyses. *International Journal of Legal Medicine,* 136(5), 1717–1736. https://doi.org/10.1007/s00414-022-02882-2.

Almehmadi, L. M., & Lednev, I. K. (2024). Stand-off Raman spectroscopy is a promising approach for the detection and identification of bloodstains for forensic purposes. *Journal of Raman Spectroscopy,* 55(2), 227–231. https://doi.org/10.1002/jrs.6609.

Anshari, R., Tsuboi, M., Sato, H., Tashiro, K., and Ozaki, Y. (2025). Raman and ATR-FTIR unmask crystallinity changes and carboxylate group and vinyl group accumulation in natural weathering polypropylene microplastics. *Sci Rep.* 15, 2518. https://doi.org/10.1038/s41598-025-85837-y.

Bazyar H. (2023).On the Application of Microfluidic-Based Technologies in Forensics: A Review. *Sensors (*Basel), 23(13):5856. doi: 10.3390/s23135856.

Bhattacharya, A., Benavides, J. A., Gerlein, L. F., and Cloutier, S. G. (2022). Deep-learning framework for fully-automated recognition of TiO_2 polymorphs based on Raman spectroscopy. *Sci Rep* 12, 21874. https://doi.org/10.1038/s41598-022-26343-3.

Bovens, M., Crutis, D., & Cuypers, E. (2019). The use of chemometrics in forensic chemistry. *Forensic Science International,* 301, 1–10. https://doi.org/10.1016/j.forsciint.2019.04.005.

Brandenburg, R. F., Verduin, J., de Ridder, R., Weesepoel, Y., Alewijn, M., Heerschop, M., Keizers, P. H. J., van Esch, A., & van Asten, A. C. (2021). Performance evaluation of handheld Raman spectroscopy for cocaine detection in forensic case samples. *Drug testing and analysis,* 13(5), 1054–1067. https://doi.org/10.1002/dta.2993.

Bruce, K. A., Arnold, D. C., Sauzier, G., & Lewis, S. W. (2024). Considerations and future perspectives for the vibrational spectroscopic analysis of forensic cosmetic evidence. Wiley Interdisciplinary Reviews: *Forensic Science*, 6(6), e1533.

Cadd, S., Li, B., Beveridge, P., O'Hare, W. T., Campbell, A., & Islam, M. (2016). The non-contact detection and identification of blood stained fingerprints using visible wavelength reflectance hyperspectral imaging: Part 1. Science & justice*: journal of the Forensic Science Society,* 56(3), 181–190. https://doi.org/10.1016/j.scijus.2016.01.004.

Chalmers, J. M., Edwards, H. G. M., & Hargreaves, M. D. (Eds.). (2012*). Infrared and Raman spectroscopy in forensic science.* John Wiley & Sons. https://doi.org/10.1002/9781119962328.

Chango, X., Flor-Unda, O., Gil-Jiménez, P., & Gómez-Moreno, H. (2024). Technology in Forensic Sciences: Innovation and Precision. *Technologies,* 12(8), 120. https://doi.org/10.3390/technologies12080120.

Chen T, Schultz ZD, Levin IW. (2009). Infrared spectroscopic imaging of latent fingerprints and associated forensic evidence. *Analyst; 134*(9):1902-4. doi: 10.1039/b908228j.

Chongtham, N., Chophi, R., & Singh, R. (2022). Discrimination of electrical tapes using ATR-FTIR spectroscopy and chemometrics. *Journal of Forensic Sciences,* 67(3), 911–926. https://doi.org/10.1111/1556-4029.14998.

Doty, K. C., McLaughlin, G. & Lednev, I. K. (2016). A Raman "spectroscopic clock" for bloodstain age determination: the first week after deposition. *Anal Bioanal Chem* 408, 3993–4001. https://doi.org/10.1007/s00216-016-9486-z.

Edelman, G. J., Gaston, E., van Leeuwen, T. G., Cullen, P. J., & Aalders, M. C. (2012). Hyperspectral imaging for non-contact analysis of forensic traces. *Forensic science international,* 223(1-3), 28–39. https://doi.org/10.1016/j.forsciint.2012.09.012.

Ewing, A. V. & Kasparian, S. G. (2017). Infrared spectroscopy and spectroscopic imaging in forensic science. *Analyst,* 142(2), 257–272. https://doi.org/10.1039/C6AN02244H.

Ganapati, K., Maram, S. S., Manikandan, V. M. (2025). Hyperspectral Imaging in Forensic Science: An Overview, Application Areas and Recent Advancements. In: Bajaj, A., Abraham, A. (eds.) Computational Intelligence Based Hyperspectral Image Analysis and Applications. *Intelligent Systems Reference Library*, vol 269. Springer, Cham. https://doi.org/10.1007/978-3-031-83127-0_6.

Gardiner, D. J. (2013). Practical Raman spectroscopy. In *Modern spectroscopy* (5th ed.). Springer.

Gatta, G. D., Mantovani, L., Bromiley, G. D. (2023). Raman Spectroscopy and Forensic Mineralogy. In: Mercurio, M., Langella, A., Di Maggio, R. M., Cappelletti, P. (eds.) Mineralogical Analysis Applied to Forensics. *Soil Forensics.* Springer, Cham. https://doi.org/10.1007/978-3-031-08834-6_5.

George, N., Singh, H., Jotaniya, R., & Pandya, S. R. (2022). Raman spectroscopy for the determination of forensically important bio-fluids. *Forensic Science International,* 340, 111441. https://doi.org/10.1016/j.forsciint.2022.111441.

Głomb, P., Romaszewski, M., Cholewa, M., & Domino, K. (2018). Application of hyperspectral imaging and machine learning methods for the detection of gunshot residue patterns. *Forensic science international,* 290, 227–237. https://doi.org/10.1016/j.forsciint.2018.06.040.

Guo, K., Shen, Y., Gonzalez-Montiel, G. A., Huang, Y., Zhou, Y., Surve, M., Guo, Z., Das, P., Chawla, N. V., Wiest, O., and Zhang, X. (2025). *Artificial intelligence in spectroscopy: Advancing chemistry from prediction to generation and beyond.* arXiv. https://doi.org/10.48550/arXiv.2502.09897.

Hakonen, A., Wu, K., Stenbæk Schmidt, M., Andersson, P. O., Boisen, A., and Rindzevicius, T. (2018). Detecting forensic substances using commercially available SERS substrates and handheld Raman spectrometers. *Talanta,* 189, 649–652. https://doi.org/10.1016/j.talanta.2018.07.009.

Harper, L., Powell, J., Pijl, E. M. (2017). An overview of forensic drug testing methods and their suitability for harm reduction point-of-care services. *Harm Reduction J.,* 14(1):52. doi: 10.1186/s12954-017-0179-5.

Huang, T.-Y., & Yu, J. C.-C. (2021). Development of crime scene intelligence using a hand-held Raman spectrometer and transfer learning. *Analytical Chemistry,* 93(26), 9335–9342. https://doi.org/10.1021/acs.analchem.1c01099.

Ifa, D. R., Jackson, A. U., Paglia, G., & Cooks, R. G. (2009). Forensic applications of ambient ionization mass spectrometry. *Analytical and Bioanalytical Chemistry,* 394(8), 1995–2008. https://doi.org/10.1007/s00216-009-2659-2.

Jackson, G. P. & Barkett, M. A. (2023). Forensic mass spectrometry: scientific and legal precedents. *Journal of the American Society for Mass Spectrometry,* 34(9), 1483–1503. https://doi.org/10.1021/jasms.3c00124.

Ka Khei L., Verma R., Tan E. L. Y., Low K. H., Ismail D., Mohamad Asri M. N. (2023). Rapid and nondestructive analysis of lipstick on different substrates using ATR-FTIR spectroscopy and chemometrics. *Journal of Forensic Sciences,* 68(3), 1001–1008. https://doi.org/10.1111/1556-4029.15223.

Kahl, K. W., Seither, J. Z., & Reidy, L. J. (2019). Validation of a comprehensive urine toxicology screen by LC-MS/MS and a comparison of 100 forensic specimens. *Journal of Analytical Toxicology,* 43(9), 734–745. https://doi.org/10.1093/jat/bkz066.

Khandasammy, S. R., Fikiet, M. A., Mistek, E., Ahmed, Y., Halámková, L., Bueno, J., Lednev, I. K. (2018). Bloodstains, paintings, and drugs: Raman spectroscopy applications in forensic science, *Forensic Chemistry,* 8: 111-133, https://doi.org/10.1016/j.forc.2018.02.002.

Kirkbride, K. P. (2000). Visible and ultraviolet spectroscopy. In J. A. Siegel, P. J. Saukko, & G. C. Knupfer (Eds.), *Encyclopedia of forensic sciences* (Vol. 3, pp. 2452–2458). Academic Press. https://doi.org/10.1016/B0-12-227215-3/00309-9.

Lee, H. L., Lin, H. J., & Yeh, T. Y. (2023). Liquid chromatography with tandem mass spectrometric method for determination of 425 drugs and poisons in dried blood spots and application to forensic cases. *Journal of Chromatography B: Analytical Technologies in the Biomedical and Life Sciences,* 1247, Article 124337. https://doi.org/10.1016/j.jchromb.2023.124337.

Lewis, S. W., Heavey, A. L., Bouzin, J. T., López, T., Sauzier, G., & Parrish, J. (2024). Frugal forensics: addressing the challenges of sustainable forensic science service provision. *Australian Journal of Forensic Sciences.* doi: 10.1080/00450618.2024.2324722.

Lidén, M., & Almazrouei, M. A. (2023). "Blood, Bucks and Bias": Reliability and bias ability of crime scene investigators' selection and prioritization of blood traces. *Science & Justice,* 63(2), 276–293. https://doi.org/10.1016/j.scijus.2023.01.005.

López-López, M., López-Ramos, D., García-Ruiz, C., & García-Campaña, A. M. (2023). Advances in the application of artificial intelligence–based spectral data interpretation: A perspective. *Analytical Chemistry,* 95(37), 13733–13745. https://doi.org/10.1021/acs.analchem.3c02540.

Mariota, K. C., Ortiz, R. S., & Ferrão, M. F. (2023). Hyperspectral imaging in forensic science: An overview of major application areas. *Science & justice: journal of the Forensic Science Society,* 63(3), 387–395. https://doi.org/10.1016/j.scijus.2023.04.003.

Mokari, A., Guo, S., Bocklitz, T. (2023). Exploring the Steps of Infrared (IR) Spectral Analysis: Pre-Processing, (Classical) Data Modelling, and Deep Learning. *Molecules,* 28(19):6886. https://doi.org/10.3390/molecules28196886.

Ntziouni, A., Thomson, J., Xiarchos, I., Li, X., Bañares, M. A., Charitidis, C., Portela, R., & Lozano Diz, E. (2022). Review of Existing Standards, Guides, and Practices for Raman Spectroscopy. *Applied spectroscopy,* 76(7), 747–772. https://doi.org/10.1177/00037028221090988.

Ntziouni, A., Thomson, J., Xiarchos, I., Li, X., Bañares, M. A., Charitidis, C., Portela, R., & Lozano Diz, E. (2022). Review of existing standards, guides, and practices for Raman spectroscopy. *Applied Spectroscopy,* 76(9), 1021–1041. https://doi.org/10.1177/00037028221090988.

OliveiraJr, E., Zorzo, A. F., and Neu, C. V. (2020). Towards a conceptual model for promoting digital forensics experiments. *Forensic Science Inter- national: Digital Investigation,* 35:301014.

Orphanou, C. M., Walton-Williams, L., Mountain, H., & Cassella, J. (2015). The detection and discrimination of human body fluids using ATR FT-IR spectroscopy. *Forensic science international,* 252, e10–e16. https://doi.org/10.1016/j.forsciint.2015.04.020.

Pavlovich, M. J., Musselman, B., & Hall, A. B. (2018). Direct analysis in real time-mass spectrometry (DART-MS) in forensic and security applications. *Mass Spectrometry Reviews,* 37(2), 171–187. https://doi.org/10.1002/mas.21509.

Proença, P., Monteiro, C., Mustra, C., Claro, A., Franco, J., & Corte-Real, F. (2020). Identification and Quantification of Antipsychotics in Blood Samples by LC-MS-MS:

Case Reports and Data from Three Years of Routine Analysis. *Journal of analytical toxicology,* 44(8), 915–922. https://doi.org/10.1093/jat/bkaa100.

Rosenblatt, R., Halámková, L., Doty, K. C., de Oliveira, E. A. C., and Lednev, L. K. (2019). Raman spectroscopy for forensic bloodstain identification: Method validation vs. Environmental interferences, *Forensic Chemistry,* 16: 100175. https://doi.org/10.1016/j.forc.2019.100175.

Saar, E., Gerostamoulos, D., & Drummer, O. H. (2010). Identification and quantification of 30 antipsychotics in blood using LC-MS/MS. *Journal of Mass Spectrometry,* 45(8), 915–925. https://doi.org/10.1002/jms.1783.

Sadler Simões, S., Castanera Ajenjo, A., & Dias, M. J. (2018). Dried blood spots combined to an UPLC–MS/MS method for the simultaneous determination of drugs of abuse in forensic toxicology. *Journal of Pharmaceutical and Biomedical Analysis,* 147, 634–644. https://doi.org/10.1016/j.jpba.2017.02.046.

Salazar-Mogollón, N. G., Quiroz-Moreno, C. D., Santana Prata, P., de Almeida, J. R., Cevallos, A. S., Torres-Guierrez, R., & Augusto, F. (2018). New advances in toxicological forensic analysis using mass spectrometry techniques. *Journal of Analytical Methods in Chemistry,* 2018, 4142527. https://doi.org/10.1155/2018/4142527.

Sharma, S., & Singh, R. (2020). Detection and discrimination of seminal fluid using attenuated total reflectance Fourier transform infrared (ATR FT-IR) spectroscopy combined with chemometrics. *International journal of legal medicine,* 134(2), 411–432. https://doi.org/10.1007/s00414-019-02222-x.

Sharma, V., Kumar, R., & Kaur, P. (2019). Forensic examination of textile fibers using UV–Vis spectroscopy combined with multivariate analysis. *Journal of Applied Spectroscopy,* 86(1), 96–100. https://doi.org/10.1007/s10812-019-00787-4.

Silva, C. S., Pimentel, M. F., Honorato, R. S., Pasquini, C., Prats-Montalbán, J. M., & Ferrer, A. (2014). Near infrared hyperspectral imaging for forensic analysis of document forgery. *Analyst,* 139(5176). https://doi.org/10.1039/c4an00961d.

Silva, R. S., Araújo, B. R. M., Cardoso, M. L. C., Cardeal, Z. L., & Augusti, R. (2024). Forensic analysis of cocaine and adulterants in banknotes by paper spray ionization mass spectrometry. *Forensic Science International,* 353, 112343. https://doi.org/10.1016/j.forsciint.2024.112343.

Sisco, E., & Forbes, T. (2021). Forensic applications of DART-MS: A review of recent literature. *Forensic Chemistry,* 22, 100294. https://doi.org/10.1016/j.forc.2020.100294.

Souza, R. R., Duarte, L. M., & Ferreira, G. B. (2025). Raman spectroscopy for forensic pen ink investigation: A review. *Analytical Methods,* 17(10), 2515–2545. https://doi.org/10.1039/d4ay01951b.

Takamura, A., Watanabe, K., Akutsu, T. et al. (2018). Soft and Robust Identification of Body Fluid Using Fourier Transform Infrared Spectroscopy and Chemometric Strategies for Forensic Analysis. *Sci Rep* 8, 8459. https://doi.org/10.1038/s41598-018-26873-9.

Tsai, P.-F., & Yuan, S.-M. (2025). Using Infrared Raman Spectroscopy with Machine Learning and Deep Learning as an Automatic Textile-Sorting Technology for Waste Textiles. *Sensors,* 25(1), 57. https://doi.org/10.3390/s25010057.

Ulery, B. T., Hicklin, R. A., Buscaglia, J., & Roberts, M. A. (2012). Repeatability and reproducibility of decisions by latent fingerprint examiners. *PLoS ONE,* 7(3), e32800. https://doi.org/10.1371/journal.pone.0032800.

Wei, Q., Zhang, M., Ogorevc, B., & Zhang, X. (2016). Recent advances in the chemical imaging of human fingermarks (a review). *Analyst,* 141(22), 6172–6189. https://doi.org/10.1039/C6AN01121G.

Wolstenholme, R. (2021). Ultraviolet–Visible and fluorescence spectroscopy. In *Analytical techniques in forensic science* (pp. 115–143). Wiley. https://doi.org/10.1002/9781119373421.ch6.

Zhou, L., Lin, X., Xie, C., Zheng, Y., & Qiu, C.-W. (2024). Miniaturized spectrometer enabled by end-to-end deep learning on large-scale radiative cavity array. arXiv. https://arxiv.org/abs/2411.13353.

Zulfiqar, M., Ahmad, M., Sohaib, A., Mazzara, M., & Distefano, S. (2021). Hyperspectral Imaging for Bloodstain Identification. *Sensors* (Basel, Switzerland), 21(9), 3045. https://doi.org/10.3390/s21093045.

Index

R

S

T

U

V

X

More information about *Walid M. Khalilia* can be found at

https://novapublishers.com/writer/walid-m-khalilia/